Rekindle the Passion While Raising Your Kids

Rekindle the Passion While Raising Your Kids

Anthony J. Garascia

 SORIN BOOKS Notre Dame, Indiana

www.sorinbooks.com

International Standard Book Number: 1-893732-34-7

Cover design by Maurine Twait

Text design by Brian C. Conley

Printed and bound in the United States of America.

Library of Congress Cataloging-in-Publication Data
Garascia, Anthony.
    Rekindle the passion while raising your kids / Anthony J. Garascia.
        p. cm.
    ISBN 1-893732-34-7
1. Marriage. 2. Interpersonal relations. 3. Married people—Conduct of life. 4. Parents—Conduct of life. I. Title.
    HQ734 .G228 2001
    306.81—dc21

                                                    2001002438
                                                    CIP

ACKNOWLEDGMENTS

I wish to express my appreciation to the following people:

Beth, my wife and partner, who provided emotional support and many helpful ideas as this book was taking shape.

Bob Hamma, for his many suggestions concerning how the concepts I wished to convey could be rendered in a more readable, more focused format; and for his respectful and careful editing of this work.

Contents

INTRODUCTION

"Live the life you've imagined," says the ad. Can you remember the life you imagined back in the days of your courtship? Are you living it now? In those days, before children, before the mortgage, even before you started planning your wedding, there was more time to talk about your life together, to dream about the future, and to imagine what your life would be someday. Now that the future has arrived, you may find it harder to carve out time for dreaming. The pressures of work, the harried pace of caring for a growing family, and the ups and downs of the daily routine can leave little time for anything but the most basic conversations about practical matters, never mind the sharing of hopes and expectations.

But when you met and fell in love and began to talk seriously about spending your future with one another, you began to form images in your minds that gave you a picture of how your life would turn out. Often, these images involved a good deal of love and unity, and provided the energy that propelled you to take the next step of proclaiming to family and friends your intent to be married. If an older family member questioned you about how you would handle future crises and problems, you probably said, "We'll work it out somehow," or,

"Our love will get us through." When two people start their married life, it's almost like they look up at the starry sky with wonder and amazement, with a mixture of gratitude and fear, but most of all with hope in the future.

This book is intended to help you continue the conversation about your relationship that started during your courtship. I hope it will enable you to sustain the original energy that propelled you forward, to marry and to begin a family together. Perhaps that energy has waned and it's time to rekindle it.

Many who work with married couples today tend to focus on helping them improve their basic skills, skills like communicating or problem solving. Such basic skills certainly are essential. But marriage is much more than a skill set. It is an act of the imagination.

Some say it is our imagination that is the uniquely human part of us. Through our imaginations we anticipate our future by dreaming about it, and the images we construct of ourselves in our future are a significant means of planning for the future. The young person who has a dream of being a doctor constructs images of what that will be like. It is usually these images that sustain the individual when the going gets tough or when the dream is tested. Sometimes we doubt our dreams and may think that our imaging has failed us. And, of course, our imagination is not based on pure fantasy but has to go through its own "reality testing" where our hopes and dreams of the future are tempered and changed by the realities of everyday life.

The idea of marriage as an act of imagination offers us a way to "remember the future." In the days of your courtship as you dreamed about the future, you didn't focus on the skills you would need to make your marriage work. You dreamed instead of being lovers, partners, companions, and friends. These images—lover, partner, companion, and friend—are the core images that serve as the organizing energy points of your marriage. These images are what sustain you when the going gets tough or when your dreams are tested. Remembering these original images can propel you to the future.

I have used these four images in my own marriage therapy with couples and can attest to the deep resonance that couples experience when they are presented with them. Each of these four images has both a secular and religious dimension and can be found in the secular literature of love as well as in the scriptures of many religions.

The four images, taken as imaginative catalysts that can sustain a marriage, can be presented as a series of propositions:

- When we marry we join together each believing the other will be with and for them a lover, a partner, a companion, and a friend.
- At every major transition in our life as a couple each of these images has to be revisited and imaged anew by us.
- All of them, taken together, will sustain a marriage. One without the others will sustain a marriage for a time but cannot alone carry a marriage into the future.
- The skills we learn that have to do with communication and problem solving are the means we use to sustain these images over time.

Imagination and spirituality go hand in hand. It is our imaginations that impel us to ask spiritual questions—questions about the meaning and purpose of life, about suffering and death, about coping with our limits and failures, our questions. And it is our imaginations that lead us to place ourselves in another's shoes and have empathy for those who suffer. As we engage in this process we draw from the spirituality that our religious traditions offer us and engage in the creation of a unique spirituality for our marriage. The spiritual source that this book draws primarily from is the Judeo-Christian tradition, although other sources are occasionally employed. We begin by focusing on the relationship between two spouses and the importance of intimacy; then we explore the four images of married love, and then move onto skills and other essential ingredients of marriage. In each chapter the spiritual dimension is brought into focus along with a few questions to prime the pump of your own spiritual imagination.

Each chapter can be read in a ten to fifteen minute period. It is my hope that this book will be read equally by men and women. The brevity of the chapters is intended to facilitate discussion between you. The chapters can also be used by small groups of married people for enrichment or discussion purposes. Each chapter has a set of questions meant to start the conversation. The aim of these questions is to offer you some positive steps you can take to make your marriage better.

Each chapter also has a "Real Life" section that presents a particular problem that a married couple might encounter. These life illustrations are fictional renderings of problems that married couples often encounter. While my experience as a marriage therapist has been helpful in knowing the territory of marriage problems, it is important to note that they are not case studies as such and no case notes were consulted in the construction of them. If you recognize your experience in any of the illustrations then I have done my job well.

Skills are important, especially during the years when your time and energy are so engaged in raising a family. And while this book will place a good deal of emphasis on these skills, I hope it will always help you to remember that marriage is more than a set of skills. More importantly, I hope it will encourage you to use your imagination to find new ways to grow as lovers, partners, companions, and friends.

1

FOCUS ON THE RELATIONSHIP

*I married the first man I ever kissed. When
I tell my children that, they just about
throw up.*

—BARBARA BUSH

In the sport of archery focus is all important. All the energies of the athlete must be focused on the bull's-eye. What
is more, there needs to be an almost perfect coordination of
the athlete's eyes, hands, and muscles as the target is found, the
arrow is drawn back on the string, and then released with pre-
cise accuracy. If the athlete is well focused, the mark will be
found.

In the Jewish scriptures the concept of "missing the mark"
was used to describe how the people lost their focus on their
relationship with God. The ancient Hebrews talked of going
wide of the mark suggesting that the people had other things
on their mind and lost sight of their relationship with God.

Today we can use the same image to begin our reflection
on marriage. A problem many of us experience is that there are
so many good things to focus on. We have our careers, the
needs of our children, volunteer activities, extended family
commitments, not to mention all the economic strain that
comes with raising a family.

In the movie *City Slickers,* Curly tells the character played by Billy Crystal that he needs to find the one important thing in life to focus on. He holds up one finger saying, "one thing." For you as a married couple, that one thing is the relationship that exists between you.

Sometimes married people forget this simple truth because of the demands of work, family, and an incredibly busy schedule. If you're like most people with families, you tend to sacrifice your needs in order to meet those of others. But if you keep putting off your needs, then you are likely to neglect the needs of your marital relationship. And like any hungry child wanting attention, your relationship will start crying and asking to be fed and cared for. It's important that you don't wait until it's too late, because any relationship can die for lack of care and attention.

In the Beginning Was the Relationship

When the two of you married you became co-creators of a new reality, your marital relationship. That's part of the meaning of the biblical phrase so often used in weddings, "The two will become one." You and your spouse took vows before friends and relatives and publicly proclaimed that you would love each other for as long as you lived. Then you went off to be congratulated at the reception, to make toasts, to sing and dance, and then on to your honeymoon. It's a marvel that human words spoken as vows can bring about a new reality that defines your life and gives it structure. The relationship that your wedding celebrated is a unique creation, dependent on both of you for caring.

What does it mean to have a marital relationship? Well, for one thing it expands the way the two of you talk about needs. Before you met and fell in love you both had individual needs, likes and dislikes. Now that you have committed to each other, you have discovered that there is a third reality. Before there were two sets of individual needs. Now there is a third need, expressed in the words "our needs." In any healthy marriage there exists a balance between "yours," "mine," and "ours." This is why we can talk about "your needs," "my needs," and "our needs."

Another way to look at your relationship is to treat it as if it were a living entity. This may seem to be strange to couples who already have two or three children and are struggling just to meet basic needs. But before you had children, way back when you fell in love, the two of you created a relationship based on trust, intimacy, communication, and friendship. And this relationship will be with you for all your married life. It preceded your children and will be with you after your children leave home to begin their own independent lives. And like all things living, your relationship needs to be cared for, fed, sheltered, and comforted when life becomes troublesome.

The relationship between you and your spouse may be something the two of you take for granted, like a trusted friend you assume it will always be there, but the thing that many of us don't realize is that there are many stresses and concerns that can begin to starve the relationship and cause it to suffer. The following represent just a few stresses that can take your attention off of your relationship with your spouse.

- a sense of being overworked with no time to relax and unwind,
- unceasing demands of job and children,
- financial concern and worry,
- a "hurdle" mentality that encourages us to see the events of life as a series of hurdles to be jumped—we jump one only to come quickly up to the next,
- a time deficit that causes us to continually sacrifice our time for the needs of others,
- the almost endless needs of our children.

All the above stresses are part of the normal ebb and flow of life. But *what we do with these stresses* is the important thing. This is why it is important for the two of you to do some planning as to how, in the midst of all the craziness of life, you will stay in touch with each other. In other words, how will you care for and feed the living entity that you call your relationship? This is not always an easy task, especially if the two of you are stressed out and overwhelmed with the demands of daily life.

THE CARE AND FEEDING OF YOUR RELATIONSHIP

All of us know instinctively what is good for us and what is good for our relationships. In my counseling with couples I ask them to identify the things that would help them build their relationship and get along better. They usually come up with the following list:

- regular "check in time," communication time,
- time to unwind individually,
- time to care for each other,
- better conflict resolution skills.

Couples almost always know what is good for their relationship, but don't always take the steps to follow through. Why not? The following are some of the reasons why; after each there is a suggested remedy for the particular dilemma presented.

1. Under stress we tend to communicate and behave in a more dysfunctional manner.

We also tend to stop doing those things that are good for us. There are, of course, people who communicate in a healthy manner when they are stressed out and overwhelmed. But for most of us, when we are under a good deal of stress we tend to focus more on ourselves and our stress levels and to blame the other person for not helping us. We may even yell, call names, storm off, pout, and "hit below the belt." When we're stressed out we often feel less in control, like we're out of options. Thus, we are less tolerant of others' foibles and mistakes.

Remedy: If the above is happening right now, each of you might draw up a list of things that you would do to relieve your stress and take care of yourself. Share this with your spouse. Notice if you have gotten away from doing good things both for yourself and for your relationship. And most important, prioritize your list and begin to do the one or two things that will help you take better care of yourselves. Empower each other and work as a team. Don't let lack of time stop you.

2. We tend to expect the other to read our mind and know what we want.

We also tend to read the mind of our spouse. This is especially true when we are under stress. Somewhere along the line many of us picked up the belief that we shouldn't have to communicate our needs, that the other person should just be able to figure them out. In the honeymoon phase of your relationship this was probably true. But as your marriage continues to evolve it's even more important to say what's on your mind.

Remedy: Say what is on your mind and what you need in a given situation. Take the risk of honesty. Get rid of the expectation that your spouse should be able to read your mind. And commit to not reading the mind of your spouse. Check in, ask questions, show you care by listening.

3. We secretly look to the other to make our self happy.

We may try very hard to make our spouse happy. And if we fail we might either get sad, angry, or a little of both. And we might begin to give up on the relationship.

Remedy: It's up to each of you to define what makes you happy. Your spouse can help you achieve your happiness, but cannot make you happy unless you choose to be happy. You might not be in charge of your external environment, but you are the captain of your internal environment. You have choices. Exercise them. And one of them is to communicate with your spouse what makes you happy.

4. We fall into patterns of giving negative feedback.

Put downs, criticisms, name calling, refusing to deal with issues are like toxic chemicals that seep into a lake.

With a little seepage the lake can eventually clean itself of the negative effects. But if there is a constant inflow of toxicity into the lake then it will eventually die. The same is true for marriage. Marriages do die from the steady flow of toxic marital feedback. Every criticism, put down, or negative interchange needs five positive exchanges to counter it. The same rule that produces positive self-esteem in children also produces positive results in marriage. Dr. John Gottman, marriage researcher and author, has demonstrated that the five to one rule is a significant predictor of successfully married couples.

Remedy: Work on the art of giving positive feedback. Specific, positive comments on your spouse's behaviors, looks, traits, etc. As management expert John Covey states: "Seek first to understand." Make the commitment to build up and you will be built up. Start with yourself, not with your spouse.

Tom and Diane have been married for ten years. Each works a full time job and they have two children, ages nine and six. They have a pretty cooperative relationship in that the household chores are shared between them, even though Diane sometimes feels that the greater part of the chores falls on her shoulders. Since they are a working couple they often find that they have a time deficit. They make it home between 5:30 and 6:30 pm. Both of their children are demanding of their time and they both try to find the time to be present to them, but it's difficult. Lately Diane has noticed that her husband is going into a "zone" where he is physically present but mentally absent. When he does this he communicates less and becomes much more self-focused. He is often not aware of how Diane perceives his "zoning out."

All of this came to a crisis when Diane had a particularly busy day and felt overwhelmed upon coming home with the kids only to find Tom watching TV. She blew up, he got defensive. Feelings were hurt and an argument ensued. Later, when they were able to calm down Diane was able to describe to Tom how his behaviors appeared to her and how his emotional absence was a problem for her. Tom in turn talked to Diane about how he was stressed from too much responsibility. He admitted that he was "zoning out." All he heard during the day was about everyone's problems, and when he came home Diane talked about the problems she was having at work.

As a result of their argument the two of them decided to spend some time talking about what happens to them under stress and what each needed in times of stress. They also recommitted to going out with each other more regularly, even if it meant having a babysitter come over and watch their kids. Both felt slightly guilty for leaving their children in daycare during the day. But they decided that spending time alone with each other was as important as spending time with their children.

When you first got married, you probably experienced high energy and good feeling toward each other. Once you settle into your marriage, and especially when you have children, there is a tendency to lose the good feeling. Marriage can become more work and less fun. Yet, with a little time and thought you can recover the good feeling. It takes a little more planning and you might resist the idea of scheduling time for emotional or sexual intimacy. But it might be worth it.

- Does the above case describe some of the real time stresses affecting your relationship?

- If you were going to treat your relationship as a living entity how would you care and feed it?

- Of the four reasons why couples sometimes don't follow through on caring for their relationship which ones are more operative in your marriage?

- What are your hopes for your relationship with your spouse as you face the next six months to a year?

THE SPIRITUAL DIMENSION:
IS GOD A RELATIONSHIP?

Christianity, Judaism, and Islam share the belief that God is one. Christianity has a unique perspective on God in that it sees God as existing in a relationship of "persons" known as the Trinity. That's a tough concept to grasp: how can God be "one" and at the same time be "three?" Suppose your own marital relationship imitated the life of God in some deeper mysterious manner. There are the two of you, but you create a relationship, a unity that gives you an identity that goes beyond the sum of your two parts.

Maybe the way you express yourselves, communicate, interact, and come together in a deeply intimate way mirrors the action of the one God in creating and sustaining the universe.

Perhaps the deepest mystery of God is that God's goodness is relationship centered, that God continually gives of the "God-force" and that this God-force spills over into manifesting what we term as the "father," the "son," and the "spirit." And what would you think if your own community making and marital expression was somehow participating in the life of the One God? Does this mean that your marriage has a mystical element to it? Maybe the unfolding pattern of your life together, with your attempt to love each other more deeply, reflects the hidden, creative God that the major religious traditions speak about. An awesome thought and a great responsibility.

2

MAKE INTIMACY A PRIORITY

Keep your eyes wide open before marriage,
half shut afterwards.

—BENJAMIN FRANKLIN

I t's a "no brainer" that intimacy is an important ingredient in making marriage work. Study after study confirms that both men and women list intimacy as a key factor in marital happiness. But here's the problem that married couples face: if everyone knows that intimacy is such an important thing in a marriage why is it so difficult to obtain? That's the million-dollar question.

Lets start with an image: suppose we say that intimacy is the water that floats the boat of your marriage. Developing the image we can say that marriage is like taking a canoe trip together down a river. The surrounding shoreline serves as the context of your marriage. As you drift or paddle by you sometimes observe a quiet pastoral setting with tree lined shores and a calm easy flowing river. Life is good. You and your spouse, in your canoe, move almost effortlessly down the river. Every once in a while you pull into shore for a break, get the picnic basket out and have some food and drink. You're so relaxed that you might even make love on a secluded beach.

But life moves on. You get back into your canoe and shove off, happy to be together. The water—in this case intimacy—is deep enough to float your boat, and its currents take you along almost without any effort. Then, things begin to change. They can change gradually or suddenly, but eventually your canoe enters rough water and both of you get more concerned about keeping your boat from getting swamped. Suddenly you realize that this canoe trip—intimacy—isn't as fun as it used to be; in fact, it can be a plain bother. Not only that, but now the two of you are shouting directions at each other, often at cross purposes. You even resort to saying things like, "That was a stupid move," and, "I can't believe you did that." Both of you become angry and hurt.

You survive the rapids and learn a few things about keeping your canoe afloat in rough water, but both of you are a little bit hurt and angry at the other for the sharp words. You drift silently for a while pondering what to do and say. Suddenly your canoe runs aground; you have reached a shallow part of the river where there is only about three inches of water and you have to get out and pull the canoe forward. You pull and pull but the water doesn't get any deeper. Again you start to argue with each other. "We should have gone down that other fork. I can't believe you wanted us to take this one." You argue about your direction, compete for control, and realize that you can't really go back. All you can do is go forward and hope the water eventually gets deeper. You begin to say to yourself, "This trip isn't as fun as I thought it would be."

Intimacy, like water, comes in all forms. Sometimes it comes to us as gentle water, soothing and sustaining. Sometimes it comes as a rainstorm, where there are problems to be faced and issues to discuss. And sometimes it feels like the intensity of a hurricane, where all you can do is try to keep your balance and take shelter. And while we all say we want intimacy in a relationship, what we really mean is that we only want the gentle sustaining intimacy where we have good feelings and low conflict. What we don't bargain for is the intimacy of honest conversation where anger and conflict are directly faced. And more than that, sometimes the intimacy seems to go away completely and we're left to pull the boat of our marriage by ourselves, not feeling very in love with the person who agreed to take the journey with us. When we encounter the scary side of intimacy, many of us want to run and avoid.

Another difficulty with the word intimacy is that men and women mean slightly different things when we use it. Intimacy is often defined as *affection, fondness, love, tenderness, experience, familiarity, understanding, closeness, friendship, coitus, intercourse, love making.* That's quite a list and covers a lot of territory. There are certain subtle nuances to the word that it's important to understand if we really want to communicate with each other in a way that is intimate. According to one study there are at least five nuances to the word intimacy that affect a married couple (Gold, J.M., "Gender and Intimacy," *The Family Journal,* 5(3), 1998, 199-203). They are:

1. Emotional intimacy

as closeness and sharing of feelings. This includes all the feelings, especially anger. In this definition closeness comes from the sharing of feelings.

2. Social intimacy

as sharing friends and social networks. This type of intimacy places emphasis on getting together with friends and associates, whether the activities be playing cards, partying, tailgating, or just a quiet evening of conversation.

3. Intellectual intimacy

as sharing of ideas and values. Does it surprise you that this type of sharing creates intimacy? Think about it. Weren't there times in college or high school where ideas really turned you on and you were attracted to people because of the ideas and values they talked about? That's what we're talking about.

4. Sexual intimacy

as sexual expression and passion. No need to expand here. This is a very obvious aspect of intimacy.

5. Recreational intimacy

as playing and having fun together. "Are we having fun yet?" Well, are you? Marriage should be a source of fun for two people. "But how can we have fun when we're sharing conflictual feelings and even anger?" Intimacy really is more complicated than we realize.

When researchers look into the difference between men and women on the topic of intimacy they come up with some interesting findings. Women tend to place a higher emphasis on understanding and acceptance, trust and commitment, caring and support, and the sharing of feelings. No surprise here. Men place higher emphasis on maintaining good feelings and harmony between the two. What this means is that when a woman wants to talk about something conflictual the first instinct of the man might be to downplay the conflict. The man means well because he is acting out of his understanding of intimacy. But the woman will often take the downplaying as avoidance and become either more angry or more hurt. Complicated business, intimacy.

Wives indicate more dissatisfaction with the emotional and intellectual aspects of marital intimacy whereas husbands report greater dissatisfaction with the social and recreational components.

What this means is that there is a tendency for wives, when dissatisfied, to feel cut off emotionally and intellectually from their husbands. They might complain to a friend that their husbands don't share their feelings and don't communicate with them as much as they would like concerning their thoughts on current events, their values, the issues at the job site, and the like.

Husbands, when dissatisfied, tend to feel that their wives do not want to participate with them as much in social activities or in social networks; they also may feel more cut off from their wives in terms of doing things together recreationally. Also important for husbands is the maintaining of harmony in the relationship.

Here, it is important to note the distinction between *having* "good feelings" or harmony and the *sharing* of feelings. While women place more emphasis on the sharing of feelings, men often get themselves into a bind when they begin to think that the sharing of what they perceive as "negative" feelings (anger, hurt, sorrow, etc.) will destroy the harmony in the relationship. If husbands could understand that the expressing and talking about "negative" feelings will build harmony between the two then they might be more willing to partake in an exchange of feelings with their wives.

What about sexual lovemaking? Recent studies indicate that this aspect of intimacy is valued just about equally between the sexes as an important part of intimacy. This may come as a surprise to some readers, due to the stereotype that suggests husbands wanting to make love more than their wives. However, there seems to be more equality between husbands and wives concerning the importance of lovemaking in the relationship. At least one researcher claims that couples who maintain a frequency of lovemaking at least once a week report a higher marital satisfaction.

Carol was twenty when her parents divorced. At the time she was a sophomore in college and she took the news quite hard. She knew that her parents had argued frequently but always assumed that they would "kiss and make up." She simply had no clue that their marriage was in trouble.

The explanation both of her parents gave her was the same: there had been no affairs and both had simply drifted apart from each other over the years. Her dad would golf regularly while her mom played tennis and had an active social life outside the home. She just never saw any of this coming.

The next few years were tough on Carol. She finished college but her grades suffered a bit. Her own sense of self-trust and self-esteem, which hadn't been all that great before her parents' divorce, now began to suffer even more. She experienced a number of quick, intense relationships with men, all of them ending abruptly and all of them causing her concern about her ability to enter into a long term relationship.

Now at age thirty-one Carol was facing her first crisis in her own marriage. She and Matt had been married for eight years and had two young children, ages five and two. Carol was beginning to feel that she didn't love Matt anymore. Their courtship had been one where Matt had been the primary pursuer. Carol had been reluctant at first and had rebuffed Matt's advances on a number of occasions. But Matt had been determined and they eventually began to date. Carol found Matt to be sensitive, caring, and organized, but conservative in his tastes and habits. While Carol liked to go out dancing or be with friends, Matt preferred a quiet evening at home. And when she would express her dissatisfaction she felt that Matt was dismissive of her point of view. It was almost as if he didn't want to talk with her, which was confusing. In the early years of courtship and marriage they had often gone for long walks and Matt seemed intensely interested in her thoughts and feelings.

The way Carol put it, there was little "pizzazz" left in the relationship. She began to wonder if she had made a mistake in marrying Matt and whether he appeared a "safe" bet to her, coming off of the turmoil created from her own parents' divorce. She knew that she was also a bit overwhelmed from being a mother of two young children and wondered if she just wasn't burned out altogether. She recently had begun losing weight and began waking up around three in the morning. All she would do was worry. She wanted to take the risk and tell her husband how she felt, but was afraid that he would dismiss her concerns again. Yet she knew that she was becoming increasingly dissatisfied.

Awareness in Action

It's easy to be completely present to someone when you're not hurried, stretched, or stressed out from the daily rhythm of life. Marriage is sometimes like a juggling act: we try to keep all the objects in the air, in balance, not dropping anything. It takes practice and discipline to live a busy, stressed existence and take time to listen to the ones we love. We need to remember that we juggle all the things of married life because they are worth keeping in the air, worth not being dropped. Maybe we need to think about being more appreciative of the things that our spouse keeps going and communicate that to him/her. At the same time we sometimes get out of touch with what first attracted us to each other.

- Are the descriptions of the ways that men and women understand the word intimacy true of you and your spouse?

- Are anger and dealing with hurt feelings the scariest part of intimacy for you? If so, what makes this either scary or difficult?

- In the above slice of life Carol was afraid to talk to Matt about her feeling that their marriage had cooled off. What prevents you from dealing with the tougher issues? Do you fear rejection?

- What is the benefit of taking the risk to deal with the tough issues?

- Finally, is there anything that you want to do differently in order to take responsibility for how you create intimacy with your spouse?

THE SPIRITUAL DIMENSION:
INTIMACY AND SPIRITUALITY

"If God were one of us, just a stranger on the bus . . ." goes a popular song. But suppose God really was one of us. Would God need to share feelings, values, and have fun together with friends?

And most important, would God be open to suffering, to getting old, to having people disappoint and not keep their word? Christianity as a religion is based on that very premise: that God is a stranger on the bus. Except that Christianity holds that God is not a stranger, but is revealed to us *in the stranger*, as well as in those we know and in our spouse.

What if each of us carries within us the "God-force," what we traditionally have called the Spirit of God? If we took this seriously would this change the way we communicated with each other? Perhaps we would value just a little deeper the intimacy that we created, knowing that it partakes in the mystery which we name as God and creator.

3

BE LIFETIME LOVERS

We practice safe sex. We gave up the
chandelier a long time ago.

—KATHY LEE GIFFORD

The image "lovers" is the easiest of the four images of married life to grasp, and is perhaps our culture's dominant image of marriage. The image of lovers is self-evident: two people share love and passion for one another, they seem almost bound like magnets. This image is emotionally charged. We often hear people talk about "falling in love," or "being swept off their feet." Some even talk about being destined for each other in a mystical way. The image of lovers naturally refers to a deep sexual connection. After all, being passionate lovers is one primary way that "two become one."

At its deepest level, there is a spiritual dimension to the image of lovers. It speaks to a sense of call to be together, that somehow the union of the two contributes to the building up of the earth and the human community. The book of Genesis speaks of the union of man and woman by saying: "It is good for the two to be together." Thus there is a spiritual affirmation of a deep and passionate love. As lovers a married couple participates in the divine energy through which God created the world. Through creative energy married lovers can say "our love is so deep and intense that we are no longer just two people, in a mystical way we have become one, a new creation."

There is an energy between lovers, a boldness that asserts that the love between the two almost impels them to take risks together that they might not as individuals. There is a felt uniqueness that is shared between the two which states in so many words: "No one but us enjoys the unity and sense of completeness that we feel." And there is a tremendous amount of energy for the relationship. Everything can seem new, even tasks that were once boring or distasteful can appear to be tolerable or enjoyable.

Living as lovers does not mean that a couple will automatically enjoy passionate sex on a frequent basis. After all, our sexual responses are as much learned over time as they are built into our biology. This is often an unrealistic expectation of many newly married couples. The frequency of sex, what gives each person pleasure, and how to achieve pleasure are often unvoiced expectations of early married life. Perhaps the most important aspect of being lovers is that the two people truly enjoy being in each others' presence, both in bed and out, and that they are committed to keeping their life as lovers strong by being passionate about communication and conflict resolution.

THE MANY SIDES OF SEX AND SEXUALITY

Let's define sex as the biological act of sexual intercourse. Obviously, it has two purposes, pleasure and procreation. Let's define sexuality as the potential sexual expression of a person who has a particular sex (male/female), a specific body type, a specific emotional makeup and a specific history. Thus, engaging in sexual intercourse in a free manner with another takes into account one's biology, body type, emotional makeup, and one's specific personal history. This specific history includes what we were taught about sex by our parents, our early sexual experiences, and whether or not we feel good about our bodies. All of this explains why it can sometimes be so difficult for married people to connect sexually with each other. The act of sexual intercourse, because it is human, is meant to be an integrated experience that takes into account one's experiences in all the above categories. If you have had a great day at work while your spouse has had a lousy day, who do you think will be in a better mood for sex?

There are four ways that sexual expression manifests itself in the course of a marriage. They are: sex as communication of emotional closeness, sex as pleasure, sex as tension reliever, and sex as obligation. It might be helpful for you and your spouse to identify if any of these views are present in your relationship.

SEX AS COMMUNICATION OF EMOTIONAL CLOSENESS

This view of sex sees intercourse as another, much deeper form of communication. As your emotional relationship goes, so goes your sex life according to this view. Sexual intercourse mirrors the extent of emotional closeness present in your relationship. If you feel this way about sex you will have a difficult time making love or being present to love making while it is occurring, if you feel out of touch with your spouse. The unspoken message is, "If I feel emotionally close to you, if we are communicating on deeper levels, then I feel more sexually attracted to you." We can communicate sexually about so many things: friendship, celebration for a promotion, happiness at an anniversary, even being scared about losing each other. A spouse who doesn't place as high of a priority on sex as communication of emotional closeness will become frustrated when the other doesn't want to make love because of feeling "out of touch."

Conversely, the spouse who sees this view as a high priority might sometimes feel that he or she has to give in to keep the other happy. Another variation on this is the fact that some spouses feel closer to their spouse *after* they have made love and can't always understand why it is they need to have emotional closeness before they make love. In their view sex is a way to achieve emotional closeness. If this is occurring in your relationship, the best thing that the two of you can do is to talk about it and surface some of the underlying issues that create tension.

SEX AS PLEASURE

Who could argue with this view of sex? It seems so simple, but consider all the things that can hamper sexual pleasure: stress, tiredness, tension between the two of you, young children who intrude upon your lovemaking, lack of time, busy schedules, job worries, kid worries, financial worries, etc. The list is long and you can probably think of many other things to add to it. But then you have to ask yourself just who is responsible for whose pleasure? Are you responsible to ensure that your spouse feels pleasure during love making? Surely, you want to please your partner. And if you don't, that will most likely cause tension between the two of you. Sex as pleasure is simple as long as you're having pleasure, but let any of the above questions or stresses intrude and things get complicated, for sure. The most important thing, again, is to talk about this in such a way that the two of you can really listen to each other without becoming defensive.

SEX AS TENSION RELIEVER

Admit it, an orgasm is fun and provides a big endorphin payoff in the brain. Our brains are considered by many experts as the primary sex organ; it's in the brain where we have our fantasies, feel attraction, and seek sexual release. And does it come as a surprise to you that one or both of you turn to sex from time to time to relieve tension? Of course, when this happens the other person can begin to feel like an object, especially if the other person thinks of sex as communication of emotional closeness. There is a cultural element to all of this too, since many men have bought the message from society that it's okay to eroticize their stress. This means that some men who are stressed will look to lovemaking to help them relieve their stress and thus get closer to their wives. Many women, on the other hand, will seek to talk about their stress with their husbands before they make love and may resent it if they think their husbands are avoiding talking and just being "horny."

Is using sex to relieve tension wrong? It doesn't have to be as long as the two of you are clarifying your expectations concerning your sexual relationship. The two of you have to create your own rules and come to them freely through discussion and understanding of one another's needs. Obviously if sex is *only* about relieving tension then you and your spouse might have some serious talking to do. But if your rules incorporate sex as communication of emotional closeness as an important item, then maybe there is some room for the relief of tension. But you have to talk it through.

SEX AS OBLIGATION

Sex as obligation does creep into a relationship over time. One of you might sometimes feel more obligated than the other. You might feel more tired and less "into it," but decide to make love anyway because you really do love your spouse. The dangerous part of sex as obligation comes when you begin to experience obligation most of the time. This is a sign that you might need to talk to someone like a marriage counselor. Or it could be a sign of your own stress and/or depression. Sex as obligation may affect your marriage, but it should not take over your marriage. Talking about it can be scary, but also very liberating. Take the risk and talk it through. That's how marriages are revitalized.

Amy and Ron have been married for eleven years. They have three children, ages ten, eight-and-a-half, and six. They would both describe their marriage as strong and both are very committed to one another. But they have struggled with a pattern in their relationship that causes both of them distress. When Ron's schedule becomes very busy his stress rises and he becomes more distant from Amy and the children. Sometimes he will work on the computer for hours without talking to her. At the same time his requests for lovemaking increase. At first Amy is ok with this, hoping that if they make love more frequently then Ron will want to talk with her more. But she feels that just the opposite occurs: Ron stays uncommunicative at the same time his physical approaches increase.

At some point in this process Amy gets quite angry with Ron's distance and they have an argument. Amy's anger is centered on Ron's emotional distance, her anger leads her to withdraw from Ron physically. The tension increases and Ron feels pushed away from Amy. Sometimes the tension ends with a big "blow out" argument that clears the air, but which leaves them both emotionally drained. At other times the tension gradually decreases as each maintains distance from the other.

During the times when there is less tension both of them have tried to understand how to break the pattern. Amy has made it clear to Ron that she finds it difficult to be sexual with him when he is emotionally distant. Ron tells Amy that sometimes he feels she uses his emotional distance as an excuse for not being physically close to him, and that there are many times when he is emotionally present to her and where she is still physically distant from him. When that occurs he feels hurt and sometimes rejected. Both realize that when the pattern plays out each of them experience hurt.

Both of them recognize the various parts of the pattern and would like to change it so that they could avoid the conflict and connect with each other on a more consistent basis. They realize that they both have different reactions to stress and different expectations about sex. Even though they are aware of all of this, they keep getting caught in the same, repeating pattern.

Maintaining sexual intimacy is an important part of married life. Your sexual life will most likely reflect the ebb and flow of your marriage. Job stress, young children, a lack of time, a lack of communication, and many other things will affect your ability to connect sexually. Often, just making a commitment to focus on the importance of your relationship is enough to restore a balance to your sexual expression.

- When was the last time that the two of you got away and really enjoyed yourselves emotionally, physically and sexually?

- What is the right mix of the four views of sex for you?

- Has your own view of sex as it pertains to your married life changed through the years? How so?

- What is the one thing you want your spouse to understand about the way the two of you engage in love making?

- What is the one thing you can do to increase the reality of the two of you being lovers for each other?

THE SPIRITUAL DIMENSION: SEXUALITY AND ECSTASY

Our sexuality is a fundamental part of being human, and being human, we realize that sex is not only about biology and reproduction but it goes far beyond biology to encompass spirituality. When you get in touch with the power of sexuality it can be an enthralling experience. You experience the body as good and discover that intimacy between you and your lover is almost limitless. When the two of you become one through love making you experience what the mystics refer to as ecstasy. You feel transcendent, in touch with the divine presence.

The root of the word ecstasy is from the Greek *ekstasis* which suggests going out of your present state. We know the word today as meaning being overtaken with joy, astonishment, almost in a trance like state. The great mystics achieved ecstasy, and went out of their normal states, through meditation and prayer. They got in touch with the divine through a focused state of prayer that led them into an ecstatic trance.

In the fullest expression of human sexual love something similar happens. You begin perhaps with seeking your own pleasure, but then move out of that state to pleasure the other. Then, in a deeper union of souls, your identity merges for a moment with the other. You and your spouse really are one community for a brief moment. And if orgasm is a physical experience, the ecstasy you feel goes far beyond the physical pleasure. And for a moment the two of you feel the pleasure and ecstasy of God.

4

WALK AS A COMPANION

When two people love each other, they don't look at each other, they look in the same direction.

—GINGER ROGERS

Companionship is another very important image for enhancing marriage. The quest for intimacy drives us to seek out someone who will be there for us in the good times and in the bad. A companion is someone who agrees to share with you, scheme with you, and dream your future with you. A companion is someone who seeks to join you in imagining what lies ahead, someone who will create a special kind of closeness with you, who will share innermost longings and secrets.

Most importantly, a companion will share your sufferings and your troubles. The effect that love can have on another is amazing. Your spouse falls in love with you, learns about your physical and perhaps psychological shortcomings and still wants to be with you because he or she loves you for who you are. Later on in life, if you face an emotional or physical hardship, your spouse is by your side, helping you cope and find solutions, not because you are a victim, but because he or she loves you and wants to embrace your troubles. A companion in marriage is the human face of God walking your walk and talking your talk, even though the walk and the talk are sometimes very troubled.

We all walk the road of life. Many times we want someone to be there for and with us. This is what marriage is all about. When a couple marry they know implicitly that they will encounter unknown surprises, both good and bad. The image of companionship reminds the couple that wherever the road goes each person does not have to walk it alone.

Life is seldom a straight and even road. It comes with all kinds of bumps and twists. We can be hurt, sometimes very deeply. We look to our spouse to help us when the messiness of life becomes too much. A crisis seems to be always just around the corner, and with it comes the fear. Will we be faithful to our chosen path? Will we continue to be companions for one another despite the messiness of our lives? What if the road becomes cluttered with obstacles and the going gets tough?

To really share a life together with someone, to be a companion, means that we will get our hands dirty. Everyone's life story has both accomplishments and leftover hurts. Now that the energy of early love has faded a bit we understand more deeply the good and the not-so-good in the person we married. The power of companionship comes from the act of expressing one's fidelity to the messiness of commitment to another. To be able to say that we will be faithful even though the future is unknown takes a certain amount of courage and trust. Whatever problems emerge we pledge ourselves to somehow find solutions.

This ideal of companionship means that as your relationship matures, you must accept each other's personality quirks and foibles. That is part of your commitment. It also means that sometimes you must confront together more serious issues that were hidden at the beginning of your marriage. For instance, a spouse confronting a drinking problem and making the choice to go into recovery is just one way that the unfinished business of life intrudes into the space of the marriage. Or perhaps some ten years into a marriage, a person begins to realize that he or she must deal with the effects of a verbally abusive family of origin. Issues like these are certainly "messy," and there is often a good deal of unresolved anger and resentment experienced. There can also be some dysfunctional behavior on the part of one or both of the spouses.

To commit to finding a way, to working out a process of recovery and reconciliation in the midst of painful discoveries or hurtful behavior patterns is part of companionship. To be a companion with someone who is hurting is perhaps one of the most significant ways we can love someone. That is why the image of companionship begins to take on more significance as a couple endures times of significant change, whether it is the change of having the first child or simply a change in jobs that requires a move to a new city.

Being companions can also create energy. In times of joy and accomplishment, the job promotion, pregnancy, graduation from college or grad school—and many others—provide us opportunities to be there and celebrate with our spouses. Celebrating the good times is all the more important when we recognize that we have been together in the bad times.

While we all appreciate companionship, there are at least two challenges we must confront: the lack of time and the failure to make companionship a top priority. Time is easy to understand as a threat. Sometimes we get so busy with our work or family activities that we simply forget to show up and be there with our spouse. The first time this happens we can be easily forgiven. The second time, not as quickly. By the third time we're beginning to form a pattern of neglect which can be deadly to the relationship. This leads into the second danger: not making companionship a top priority. When the crisis occurs this is what we will hear from our spouse: "you're never around, you're always busy doing other things. I wonder if you love me."

The remedy: make time to be a companion, discover what's blocking you from getting closer, be honest, talk it through. Declare your love for one another, even though it's not easy and get help if you need it. Believe that your relationship with one another is truly unique and thus worth working on and saving. Trust in God, role up your sleeves and get your hands dirty with the messiness of your love for one another and commitment to each other.

A SLICE OF LIFE

Pam and Terry have just been through the marital equivalent of a major earthquake, yet somehow their marriage has survived. Terry just recently has entered recovery and now openly admits that he has a drinking problem. He now describes himself as a "recovering alcoholic." Just two years ago he resisted the thought that he even had a problem with drinking. Both can remember the screaming matches they had over Terry's drinking, and how their three children would often place themselves in the middle of the fights just to interrupt them.

One day Pam said very clearly to Terry, "I love you and want to be your life's companion. But you have to decide whether you love me or your drinking. It can't be both." Terry had made several previous attempts to control his drinking. He had even entered an intensive outpatient recovery program. But each time he gradually resumed his drinking.

This time, however, was different. He sensed an urgency to Pam's statement and knew that he might lose his marriage. He returned to Alcoholics Anonymous and began in earnest his recovery. He stated to Pam that he didn't want his marriage to break up. Pam didn't want the marriage to end either; she was hopeful that Terry's drinking days were over.

Now that Terry is moving into recovery they both realize that there is much damage to their relationship that needs to be repaired: trust that was broken, threats that were made, and even Pam's fear that Terry might one day resume drinking are just a few of their present issues. Both were scared about repairing the damage yet both stated that they had been through too much to call it quits now. So they tell themselves that somehow they will finish the project of their marriage that they began some fifteen years ago.

Awareness in Action

Sometimes we don't feel that our spouse is "there for us." Sometimes we have to take the risk of asking him/her to work with us to be a more complete companion. We have to acknowledge that sometimes there are hurts and fears that keep us from experiencing a deeper companionship with our spouse. We may have to realize that we have unrealistic expectations. We might have to challenge ourselves to be a more complete companion. The mirror of marriage has two faces.

- Have there been times when you really came through for your spouse in times of pain or sorrow?
- Were there times when your spouse was present to your own pain and sorrow?
- Are there real hurts that prevent the two of you from becoming deeper companions in the journey of life? What are they?
- How can you move beyond them to a deeper reality of marriage?
- In the above slice of life alcohol abuse was part of Pam and Terry's "messiness." What defines the "messiness" of your life situation that, if worked on could bring the two of you together?

THE SPIRITUAL DIMENSION:
GOD AS THE UNSEEN COMPANION

When the going gets tough we often look to be rescued, and when truly bad things happen to us—like illness or the death of a loved one—we often feel abandoned by God. Why do innocent people suffer, sometimes greatly?

God does not rescue us from bad situations, but can turn those bad situations into moments of revelation to us. Instead of God as rescuer think of God as a companion who walks with you in the good times as well as bad. A companion doesn't take away your pain as much as be present to your pain. And in the being present the pain—along with the person—is often transformed. Maybe that is how God works in our lives.

There is a story in the Gospel of Luke about the disciples on the road to Emmaus shortly after Jesus was put to death by crucifixion. They were grief stricken and scared. Unknown to the two of them Jesus begins to walk with them as a stranger. He is present to their pain, to their own agony. And as they walk he helps them interpret their experiences so that they finally recognize him as their friend (Lk 24:13-35).

In a way God walks with us as the hidden companion, not taking away our pain, but being present to us, helping us interpret all the many experiences that sometimes just don't make sense.

5

BE YOUR SPOUSE'S
BEST FRIEND

Love is a fruit in season at all times.

—MOTHER TERESA

Married couples who have been married for some time often refer to their spouses as their best friends. Many of us have best friends from childhood, best friends from work, or best friends from some other social setting. But the friendship that develops between two married people is a special and unique friendship that takes in the qualities of all our other friendships yet goes much deeper. That's why the image of friendship or soul mates is so important in marriage.

With the image of friends or soul mates, there emerges a sense of a deep commonality of values, ways of thinking and feelings between the two of you. Couples who are friends know almost instinctively how the other thinks and can anticipate the other's needs. There is often an intense energy that exists on the intuitive level, the deep bond shared between the two that can appear almost psychic. Here, the commonality of feelings and values is what brings the friendship into existence. It's common for friends to share similar feelings about an experience. Empathy for the other also runs deep in this image.

Empathy means to have deep feelings for what another is going through, be that a happy or sad occasion. To say that one's spouse is a friend implies that he or she is the first person to be consulted in major decisions or happenings, and even in the every day unfolding of life.

It is curious to note that many marriages are the result of spouses becoming friends first and then, only after a period of courtship, lovers. This is true of marriages where the two people knew each other from high school or perhaps met in college, but didn't date for some time. Sometimes, when romantic love begins to intrude on best friends, there is fear that the friendship will be lost or destroyed by the shift. It is possible, however, to be both lovers and friends.

Many times a marital friendship begins to grow stronger after the early years, with their inevitable transitions and crises, have been endured. This can be true for those marriages where the image of lovers has been stressed in the early part of the marriage. This is not to say that the couple are no longer lovers; rather, as time goes on the commonality of values, feelings, and instincts begins to deepen the bonds of friendship between them. And to some extent the couple even goes beyond the parameters of friendship to a much deeper, almost mystical union that can best be described as soul mates. This is a condition where the couple can almost feel their two identities forming a deep unity, which is best described in the quote from scripture: "The two shall become one."

WHAT SUSTAINS A FRIENDSHIP?

Friendships are often built on four important foundations, *fun or enjoyment centered on common interests, meaning centered on common values, emotional support,* and *time.* All four of these are present in a marriage as in any other friendship. It's just that in a marriage a couple will often share much more deeply and exclusively than with other friendships and will have established rules concerning what knowledge of the other is allowed to be shared with friends and acquaintances. In fact, one of the early transitions that a couple often has to make is to realize that the friendship of marriage exists on almost a sacred level, and that each spouse is called to a deep loyalty to the marital friendship. The early crisis of friendship usually centers on one spouse feeling that the other has been unfaithful or disloyal to the friendship by sharing intimate information with other friends, family members, or coworkers.

In order for a marriage to stay healthy the two of you need to work on maintaining your friendship with one another despite all the pressures of parenting, jobs, extended family, and whatever personal difficulties you may be experiencing. By focusing on the four foundations of friendship you will be able to weather the stresses of early and mid-marriage and will discover that your commitment to each other deepens over time.

Fun or Enjoyment Centered on Common Interests

When was the last time the two of you had any fun? Children, as you well know, require a lot of your time, attention, and energy. This can take a toll on your relationship with each other if you are not careful. When you dated and fell in love you probably did things that were fun and energizing. Now that you have moved into the child rearing years, it's more difficult to continue to do the things that you know you both enjoy. But inevitably, there comes a time when you have to face the fact that your life together is more work and less play; getting back to having regular dates with each other is an intervention you will be glad you made.

What are your common interests? Are the two of you doing the things that you used to do when you courted? Or has the business of family, work, and children's activities taken you away from what previously sustained your relationship?

Meaning Centered on Common Values

Deep friendships are not only fun, they also bestow a sense of purpose and meaning to our lives. This is because they are based on a common set of values which gives the friends opportunity to discuss how they see the world, relationships, and the wider issues affecting their world. Part of your attraction to each other was based on admiring certain values and principles in the other. These meaning generating values can become tarnished and rusty if they are neglected due to the hassles of work, parenting, and other commitments. It's important to nourish your souls by giving yourselves the time to check in and deepen your common values. This can be done through gathering with like-minded friends, involvement in a church or other volunteer group, or by attending talks, plays, or movies which sustain, challenge, and deepen your value system. Whatever you do, the most important thing is that you continue this practice as your marriage grows and matures.

Even though friendships are formed around common values, married couples often neglect to surface these values and talk about them. You know that you are on the level of values when you can tell your spouse what you admired the most about him or her when you first met and fell in love. It's still a good idea to revisit the values that originally united the two of you.

Emotional Support

A good friend is priceless. This is the person to whom we will turn when we are down, have a problem, or are just frustrated with the day's hassles. The challenge of married life is for the two of you to continue to give emotional support to each other, despite all the stresses of your present life. One reason why marriages run into trouble is that the marital friendship has been damaged either by lack of attention, constant and unresolved conflict, or the two spouses getting busy with careers and going their different ways. It's much easier to be there for our spouse in good times. But let the stress and strain of life increase and we experience the tendency of me first: "You care for me first then I'll care for you. If you don't care for me first, then I won't care for you and might even retaliate against you." The best remedy for this kind of thinking is to build in frequent, almost daily times to check in with each other. Some people go for walks, some sit down at the end of the day and have a cup of tea, some sit on the couch together while the kids are doing something else. It doesn't have to be very long, maybe fifteen to twenty minutes, but it will return great dividends in later years because your friendship will have been nourished and fed.

Time

Time is our friend, but time can also be our enemy. It is our friend when we realize that it is not an inexhaustible resource but a precious gift. It becomes our enemy when we think we have plenty of it; that we can always get back to repairing a damaged relationship. Many couples back themselves into serious marital trouble by thinking that time alone will heal all wounds. In fact, only two people facing each other and taking responsibility for their relationship can bring about this type of healing. Just as any close friendship can whither away due to neglect, a marriage can slowly but surely starve because of time not taken to sustain the friendship.

Mary and Mike had just bought a car through an online used car dealership. They had to travel about eighty miles to pick the car up. On their way back Mike drove part of the way. As he was getting tired he decided to pull over and so that Mary could drive. Since they were in a rural part of their state of North Carolina he decide to pull over on one of the exit ramps.

He parked the car on the shoulder of the ramp, got out of the car and walked around the front to take his place in the passenger's seat. Mary walked around the back of the car. As she was walking toward the back of the car she noticed another car exiting onto the ramp. This car looked to her to be very close to the shoulder of the road. She continued to walk around the car and was just beginning to turn to walk toward the front door when she looked up again at the car that was exiting. By now it was almost on top of her and she thought to herself that she was going to be hit. She jumped back towards the shoulder and in an instant the exiting car side swiped their newly purchased car, causing damage all the way down the left side.

Mike, by now getting into the passenger seat, felt the car shake from the impact and immediately thought of his wife, who he thought had been hit by the other car. Shouting, "Mary" he leaped out of the car and ran back to find Mary shaken but not hurt. The other car went some distance, then stopped. A young man got out, dazed and shaken. He had apparently fallen asleep for a brief moment and had lost control of his vehicle.

Both Mary and Mike were shaken badly, realizing that a near tragedy had been averted. Their new car was totaled and they had to rent a car to make it home. They drove home in silence. But they held hands, each thinking of the value of their relationship and friendship with each other the past twenty-three years, and how a fluke accident almost wiped out their relationship. Later, both talked about trying to appreciate their relationship more. They both vowed to try to be more present to each other and to let the daily squabbles run off their backs.

We sometimes take our friendships for granted even when our relationships are strong and healthy, as in the case above. Has anything similar ever happened to you, where you became more appreciative of your relationship?

- Do you generally feel that you and your spouse are friends?
- What makes your friendship stronger, what blocks it from achieving its full potential?
- Do you and your spouse have as much fun as you used to?
- Are the two of you engaged in meaningful dialog with each other and in outside activities that give the two of you meaning?
- Can you turn to your spouse for emotional support? What blocks this from happening more frequently? Is time a factor?
- Finally, what can you do to take responsibility for your friendship growing and becoming deeper over time?

THE SPIRITUAL DIMENSION:
FRIENDSHIP

In the New Testament Jesus paid his disciples the highest compliment by calling them "friends" (Jn 15:15). And in the beginning of the book of Genesis, before they sinned, God had an intimate relationship with Adam and Eve. We find that God moved about the garden on a daily basis, and it seems almost as if Adam and Eve took daily strolls with God, their friend.

The original unity present in the Garden of Eden was shattered, of course, by mistrust and dishonesty. The same dynamic plays out in our marriages today. We build our friendship through honesty, sharing, and trust; we harm and sometimes destroy relationships by dishonesty, deceit, and disrespect of the other.

And of course, all special friendships are tested eventually by the crisis of betrayal. The betrayal can be big or small, but when it first comes it hurts, often very badly. But a friendship doesn't have to stop due to betrayal; sometimes a friendship becomes deeper. This is often a major test for a marriage, and many marriages have survived major hurts to the relationship by the couple doing the hard work of reconciliation.

Maybe friendships are like old, gnarled trees that are shaped by the forces of storms and winds that whip and threaten to topple the tree. But the tree grows and forms over time a tough foundation. The gnarls represent the crises that threatened the tree but which eventually led to its rugged beauty. Even the crises of friendship can make a marriage a place of rugged beauty.

6

KEEP YOUR PARTNERSHIP STRONG

Any husband who says, "My wife and I are
completely equal partners," is talking about
either a law firm or a hand of bridge.

—BILL COSBY

A partnership is usually associated with financial and legal institutions where there is a very well defined contract that describes the duties, responsibilities and benefits of a person in the partnership. Marriage is a partnership too in at least three ways:

- Marriage is an economic and legal partnership;
- Marriage is a partnership of roles, responsibilities and values;
- Marriage is a partnership of parenting and child rearing.

There are many benefits to the partnership, but problems can arise when couples don't adequately voice their expectations concerning how tasks and roles will be divided as circumstances change.

Marriage as an Economic and Legal Partnership

This is an aspect of marriage that is often taken for granted and overlooked until there is trouble in the relationship. We all know instances of bitter divorces when a couple has to split up a partnership which has both legal and financial dimensions. This can be quite painful and gut wrenching. Property settlements, pension plans, child support payments and the like all serve as a reminder that marriage, no matter the extent of happiness present, is an economic and legal partnership.

Of course, there are good reasons why a couple embarks on this sort of partnership in the first place. Facing an uncertain financial future can be a daunting task, and given that two people declare their unending love for one another, marriage can appear as a safe haven which provides them both an opportunity to plan for and to create security into their near and long term future. When you married each other, you agreed "to have and to hold, from this day forward. . . ." What is unsaid but very true is that you also committed to "plan and to implement as best we can our dreams for our future." This is why the economic and legal partnership is brought about in the first place.

Marriage as a Partnership of Roles, Responsibilities, and Values

When two people marry they bring into the marriage certain expectations about what each person will contribute to the marriage. These expectations are often very much down to earth and concrete and center on things like who will do the laundry, who will balance the checkbook, who puts out the garbage, and so on. Also included in this list is a general expectation of what each person needs from the other when things aren't going so well. For instance, the first time one spouse gets sick with the flu usually brings out unvoiced expectations of the other spouse concerning what the flu-ridden spouse needs at that particular time. Some of us revert to a childlike state, others may become cranky, while still others go into themselves and hibernate until the sickness passes.

It goes without saying that many of our expectations about the roles and responsibilities that our spouse will assume are often unvoiced before the actual wedding date. The reality of how someone actually behaves is only truly appreciated when the moment is upon us. The issue of housework, for instance, may be raised before one is married with both spouses sincerely expressing a desire to pitch in and help out.

What then accounts for the surprise and sometimes shock when one spouse finds him/herself doing the brunt of the household cleaning on Saturday morning? Most likely this occurs because our good intentions sometimes run ahead of our actual behavior, which for many of us exists on the level of habit and routine. Whatever the reason, what we say does not always match what we do.

More importantly, a marriage represents a partnership of values which form the basis of the roles we adopt and the responsibilities we assume. Spouses who share equally in household chores, for instance, do so because of the underlying value of equality. Your attraction for each other began, most likely, not only as a physical attraction but as an attraction to the values that each of you embodied. These values need to be affirmed and celebrated throughout your marriage. It's not hard to lose sight of them in the hustle and bustle of married life.

MARRIAGE AS A PARTNERSHIP OF PARENTING AND CHILD REARING

The transition from being a childless couple to having a child no doubt brought about changes in your marriage. Some couples refer this as BC (before children) and AC (after children) because it seems like the life before and after is so clearly demarcated. Consider some of the before and after changes in the following list.

Before children	After Children
A couple can sleep in on weekends.	A couple is usually up by 6 or 7 a.m.
A spouse is accountable only to the other.	A spouse is now accountable to two people.
A couple could go out at will.	A couple has to find childcare to go out.
Lovemaking is defined by the needs of the couple.	Lovemaking is defined by the needs of the child.
A couple can sleep through the night.	One or both of you are up frequently in the night.
Leisure and fun are much easier to do.	Leisure and fun are more restricted.
Laundry for two.	Laundry for three.

Perhaps you could make an even longer list! There's no doubt that many things change after the birth of the first child. Even more come with the second and third child! And with these changes often come unexpected ways of responding. For instance a husband might assume that his wife is going to get up in the middle of the night because she is breast feeding their child. The wife, on the other hand, might have the expectation that the husband will help her out by going to get their baby, changing the diaper and then bringing the baby to the wife. If these expectations are not talked about, tension will begin to escalate.

Staying on Track: Dealing With Transitions

A partnership can fail over time if it is neglected and taken for granted. That is a sad thing, but it doesn't have to happen for the two of you if you commit to keeping your partnership on track. The best way to do this is to be aware that in every major transition you will go through you have to rethink how your partnership is lived. Any transition will cause a shift in your roles, responsibilities, and perhaps even your values. If you let the pace and intensity of the particular transition control you, then you may forget to renew your partnership. This is often what happens in the divorces that occur with "empty nest" couples. A couple, married some twenty to thirty years, watches the last child leave only to realize that their marriage was organized more around the children than the two of them. When did that occur? At no particular time, but gradually as the children grew. The important thing to remember is that if a couple checks in on a regular basis, with each major transition that occurs in the family, then their own partnership will be continually renewed and affirmed.

Transitions come in all shapes and sizes. The first year or so after marriage can be a tough transition, when your expectations begin to adjust to the realities of every day married life. The first child is a major transition, as is a geographic move for a job. Promotions, losing a job, career changes are other major transitions. Children going to kindergarten, middle school, high school and off to college are major transitions. And of course, there are the much tougher transitions like major health problems, the loss of a parent or close friend to death, a miscarriage, or even the death of a child. All of these transitions can cause a couple to lose focus and get off track.

You can stay on track with the partnership of your marriage by remembering to:

- Check in with each other concerning expectations, roles, and responsibilities whenever you go through a major transition.
- Talk about and define further the core values of your relationship so that you understand that these values actually form the basis of your partnership.
- Realize that while much of your partnership will be devoted to child rearing you need to plan for the days when your children will be gone. Take the time now to spend time renewing your relationship. Don't wait until the children are gone.

Genny sat in church and quietly cried. She kept her tears to herself, carefully wiping them away with a tissue. If anyone around her noticed her tears they at least respected her need for silence. It had been nine months since her marriage of twenty-eight years to her husband had ended, first in a separation and then in a divorce. She was still at a loss to understand what had happened. Her husband had come to her about a year ago and told her that he wanted a separation. She was able to persuade him to enter marriage counseling with her, but as the counseling progressed she could tell that her husband just wasn't into it. Finally, out of exasperation with him she told him that she didn't want him to keep on coming to counseling just to please her. Shortly after that he stopped the counseling and then filed for divorce.

There had been no affair and no real warning signs to tell her that her marriage was in danger. Looking back on things she could now say that she had noticed that their relationship had cooled down a bit. They both had their own routines: she would go to a weekly bookclub, he to golf on Saturday with his friends. Once a week they went out to eat together and on the weekend usually got together with one of their two children and grandchildren. When their children were in grade school and high school they both split up the duties of attending various school events. When the last child left she noticed a gradual lessening of their own interaction with each other, but attributed this to the business of each of their lives. Their sex life, while not as passionate as it once was, was still ok, or at least she thought it was. And where in the past they would fight more, in recent years they fought less, choosing instead to refrain from "pushing each other's buttons." Looking back she knew there were flaws; she just didn't think the flaws were fatal.

When she pressed her husband to explain what went wrong, the best he could tell her was that they had slowly drifted away until one day he woke up and told himself that he wasn't in love with her anymore. Almost on a daily basis for the first four months she woke and asked herself, "How can this have happened to me?" She could come up with no satisfactory answers. She was adjusting, however slowly, to living alone, still shell-shocked from the events of the past year.

AWARENESS IN ACTION

The above case presents the sadness that can come from a marriage ending in a painful divorce. Yet the reality that marriages sometimes end the way this one did might cause the two of you to ask yourselves some deeper questions. While this is sometimes not an easy task it may be well worth the time it takes to be open to re-imaging your marriage as it moves through time. The benefit is, of course, that you both will be in much greater control of defining and attaining your own happiness.

- Does it make sense to you that the way the two of you handle the major transitions in your marriage is important to your future happiness?

- And that the two of you, in order to renew your marriage, have to re-image how it is you will be friends, lovers, companions, and partners as you weather the many transitions you face?

THE SPIRITUAL DIMENSION: PARTNERSHIP

God, it seems, wants to partner with humanity in transforming the world into the best possible place where justice and peace are primary values. Christianity as a religion places a high value on the fact that God is made human in the person of Jesus. God doesn't do the work all alone but relies on all of us to do our part. The image of walking with us on our road is a comforting one, for sure.

But one doesn't need to be a Christian in order to resonate with the image of the divine partnering with humanity. This image seems to be embedded in most world religions. And it speaks to the interdependence of all of life on earth, where all species play a part in the makeup of the living planet. Perhaps marriage, when at its best, reflects not only the divine partnering with humanity but also that of the earth partnering with humanity to continually evolve and grow.

7

COMMUNICATE EFFECTIVELY

*I can't get along with my wife—she
understands me.*

—HENNY YOUNGMAN

If communicating effectively was all that easy then there wouldn't be an entire industry devoted to helping people communicate in the workplace and home. Perhaps the two biggest areas needing improvement that couples consistently cite have to do with the quality of communication that exists in the relationship and the way that spouses solve their conflicts. In the final analysis, good communication between spouses paves the way for effective conflict resolution.

We learn how to communicate from our own families and from the friends we get to know growing up. The family is the first learning laboratory for a lot of interpersonal skills that we will later take to our adult relationships. But there is another layer of influence that we need to pay attention to: culture. It has a pervasive influence on how our communications are shaped.

Deborah Tannen, the author of *You Just Don't Understand* (Ballantine Books, New York, 1990), makes the point that in our culture men and women have been taught or "inculturated" to view information from two very different perspectives. And information about one's life, from the day-to-day goings on to the emotional states we might be experiencing, is the life-blood of the marriage relationship. Tannen suggests that women generally use information to build rapport with others while men generally view information as something to report about to someone higher up in the work hierarchy. Men, according to this view, will be more willing to give crucial information to their boss and less willing to give information to their peers.

This is why, according to Tannen, there is sometimes tension at the end of the day when husbands and wives try to talk. The wife, who sees information as something to be shared with those she trusts, even down to the details, asks, "How was your day?" But instead of being met with a full, detailed description, is only given an abbreviated "bulleted" list of events by her husband. "I got to work, we had a meeting, I had lunch with Joe, then I made of bunch of phone calls to my clients." This exchange leads to the oft-repeated remark, "He doesn't communicate with me." What the woman is actually saying is, "I want to hear more about his day, what happened, and how he feels."

Part of the above dynamic, if it operates in your relationship, might have to do with the fact that the husband is unconsciously hearing a request of a superior when asked for information. Of course, we consciously know that our spouse is not our boss, but sometimes we react on the unconscious level to these legitimate requests for information. Both spouses need to keep in mind that each person brings to the discussion different approaches to communication. Husbands need to look carefully at whether information sharing is really organized in a hierarchal manner in their worlds. In other words, do you flinch when your wife asks you for information, and if you do, is it because you really don't want to "report to your wife"? Once you can identify this you can talk about it and move beyond this negative dynamic.

Another important thing to remember is just how complex communication between two people really is. We often forget this and assume that communicating is something done rather easily. Take some time and look at how most communications happen. The process explains why even simple communications between spouses escalate into arguments.

THE PROCESS OF COMMUNICATION

1. Sender:

The one who communicates a message:

*   Communicates at between 100 and 120 words per minute.
*   Sender's communications influenced by:
    beliefs about how the world works and how people act,
    attitudes toward the future and one's expectations for an outcome,
    generalizations and assumptions about people's behaviors and their motives,
    stereotypes: rigid generalizations attached to a specific group of people.

2. Sender Communicates Meaning Through:

*   **verbal** content: what is actually said,
*   **body posture:** facial expressions and body position that communicate a feeling message (I'm angry, tense, excited, happy, etc.),
*   **voice tone:** voice tonality also communicates feelings of happiness, anger, frustration, sadness, etc.

3. Listener:

The one who receives the message and interprets meaning:

- Picks up on only 7% of a message communicated through actual verbal content.
- Gives special importance to how the message is communicated through body posture and voice tonality.
- The listener's inner self-talk happens at a rate of 600 words per minute compared to the sender's rate of speech of around 100 words per minute.
- The listener filters what is heard through his or her beliefs and themes about himself or herself and the sender. These beliefs and themes have to do with unresolved meta-issues like inclusion/exclusion, dominance/submission, power/powerlessness, belonging/rejection, respect/disrespect. This is why the listener pays special attention to voice tonality and body posture.

4. Tendency for the Listener to React Before the Sender Is Finished Speaking.

- The listener has an immediate **feeling reaction** about what he or she is hearing based on how he or she interprets the sender's communication.
- The listener tends to listen to the initial parts of the sender's communications before his or her own inner self talk takes over.
- The listener tends to read the sender's mind, thinking that he or she knows what the sender is saying before it is actually said.
- If there are any unresolved "meta-issues" in the listener's life there is an increased tendency for these to become "hot buttons" that the listener allows to be pushed.
- The listener quickly becomes a sender. The sender quickly becomes a listener. There is a built in tendency for miscommunication and arguments to develop.

Sending and Listening

The process above breaks down communication into a sending and receiving part. In reality, when we communicate we oscillate rapidly between being a sender and receiver. That's why it's so hard to really communicate and listen to the other person. Not only that, but the way we communicate is influenced by so many things, like our beliefs about the world and other people. Add to that the fact that we don't really communicate with just words, but with our entire bodies, and you can begin to see that there is a lot going on in a communication. Couples who have a lot of tension in their relationship will tell you that they often communicate better with one another and actually listen to the other when they talk on the phone. Why is this so? Because a phone conversation filters out one of the major ways we communicate, that of body posture, which includes dirty looks, frowns, and the like.

Inner Self-talk

Another thing that goes on in a communication is that we know that the sender communicates at around a 100 to 120 words-per-minute rate. But if you're the listener, your own inner self-talk is zipping by at around 600 words per minute. And that inner self-talk has to do with responding immediately to the first words out of the other's mouth. In order words, you forget to listen to the whole communication and start responding. If you're a man, there is a higher probability that you will interrupt your spouse before she is finished speaking. This is because of the rapid rate of your internal dialog.

The Meta-issues

Another thing that makes communication really tough is that we all carry around in us deeper issues and messages about ourselves, what we will call meta-issues. These are the left over themes from our childhood that never quite got resolved. They are the larger, deeper identity issues that define what gives us meaning and also what we fear the most. Themes like, inclusion/exclusion (am I in or out?), dominance/submission (am I on top or on the bottom?), power/powerlessness (do I have power and competence or am I powerless?) and safety/insecurity (am I safe or in trouble?). Meta-issues have to do with arguments that get started that really aren't about the superficial content, but often point to deeper issues in the relationship.

These meta-issues are questions we bring to any conflictual situation and they represent our worst fears about the future of our relationships. Not all of us have the same deeper issues. It's up to you to figure out which deeper meta-issues shape your agenda of listening. When we have conflict with someone we listen at an unconscious level to hear if the other person is seeking to attack us where our worst fears reside. So, if I fear exclusion, I will listen to see if any of your language about me seems exclusive. And if I perceive you're trying to exclude me then my fear will start to rise and I will respond by trying to protect myself. When I do that I will flip quickly to become a sender and attack your meta-issues, without meaning to of course. And thus the conflict begins to escalate, some times quite rapidly.

STEPS TOWARD EFFECTIVE COMMUNICATION

So how do we really communicate with another, and really listen to our spouses? The following five steps are meant to help you begin the process.

1. Drive out distractions:

When listening, focus your attention on the sender. Turn off the TV or radio. Look at the person in the eye and give him or her the benefit of your care and attention.

2. Turn down your inner self-talk:

Imagine that there is a dial on you from 0 to 10. At 10 your inner self-talk is going at 600 wpm. Can you turn down the dial so that you reach a level of around 200 wpm or less? If you can, you'll be surprised at how well you will be able to listen.

3. Make the unconscious conscious:

This is true for any of the deeper meta-issues which affect you right now. Talk to your spouse about them. Let him or her know that sometimes some of your deeper fears get touched when you communicate with one another. Chances are your spouse is not meaning to touch these fears and will be aware of them next time around.

4. Check things out, don't assume, don't think you can mind read:

Check out assumptions. Ask the other if a scowl, for instance, really means that he or she is angry with you. Don't interpret another's non verbal communication and act. Check it out first.

5. Place your emphasis on listening:

We all want to be heard and find our voice. But if everyone talks first then there will be no one to listen. Practice the art and gift of listening with your spouse.

A Slice of Life

Carolyn and George had been married for three years and they recently had a baby girl. Carolyn had decided to take maternity leave from her work for three months. She hadn't yet decided whether she would return on a full or part-time basis. At first she enjoyed the time at home with their new baby. But then, as the weeks went by, she began to miss the companionship and stimulation that she got from being at her work. She also began to depend more on George for emotional stimulation and nurturing.

George was going through some tough transitions at work and his own stress level was rising. He tried to be present to Carolyn when he came home from work and felt that he did a pretty good job of listening. But there were times when Carolyn felt that George didn't really want to hear about how her day went and she felt a bit discounted now that she had the unglamorous job of childcare. She sometimes noticed that George's attention would drift when she would tell him about her day. When this occurred she felt ignored and excluded. She would get angry with George when he got distracted. George felt that he was in a no-win situation, that try as he might he couldn't meet Carolyn's need to talk with him.

After about three months of struggling with the issue of being present to one another things started to get a bit better. Carolyn was able to return to work on a part-time basis, which gave her an opportunity for adult conversation with others. She became aware of how difficult it was to rely on George for "adult" contact. She also became aware of how difficult the transition to parenting had been on her. She also became aware that she was both afraid and angry that George wouldn't love her as much because she gave up an influential job to stay home with their baby. She realized this was her own fear of inadequacy, but she still felt vulnerable in talking to George about this issue. But they both made the commitment to talk things through no matter whether feelings were hurt. Both valued their friendship with one another and wanted to keep things on track.

Awareness in Action

The above scenario presents a deeper meta-issue in Carolyn's life—that of being ignored and excluded—that affected her relationship with her spouse.

- Are there similar deeper issues in each of your lives that sometimes affect the way you communicate with each other? Can you name them?
- What is the most difficult part of being a receiver/listener for you?
- What can you do differently and better to improve the way you listen to your spouse?

The Spiritual Dimension: Communication

One of the most important characteristics that sets humanity apart from the rest of the created world is the development of language. Certainly, other species have developed methods of communicating between themselves: birds sing, wolves howl and prairie dogs thump with their tails. All of these are forms of communication, but we humans have made communication a sophisticated art form, from cave walls, to billboards, to books and now computers.

Teilhard de Chardin, a great scientist-theologian of the twentieth century, held that love was the language of the universe. There are other scientists that speak of the universe as one large information system which seeks ever increasing levels of complexity. But suppose de Chardin is on to something, that somehow the energy that is love actually created the universe and now seeks to communicate and express itself not only through matter, but through the human community. This is what the Gospel of John is suggesting in its opening words, "In the beginning was the word. . . ." It's all about communication, about information, but most importantly about the communication of love. Do our own words build a world where love is present?

8

KNOW HOW TO SOLVE PROBLEMS

To keep your marriage brimming,
with love in the loving cup,
whenever you're wrong, admit it;
whenever you're right, shut up.

—OGDEN NASH

One bumper sticker says: "Jesus is the answer." Another reads: "What's the question?" A third: "What's the problem?" Still another: "If you're not part of the solution you're part of the problem." A visitor from another planet, upon reading these four sayings might conclude that we Americans are fixated on problem solving. Yet with all this focus why do we have so many problems? Go figure.

Married couples know instinctively that effective conflict resolution skills are an important part of a successful marriage. Surveys continually cite poor conflict resolution as a major cause of marital breakdown. So it makes sense that the better able the two of you are to solve problems in a timely fashion the happier your marriage will be. Easier said than done, but perhaps easier to accomplish than you realize.

Successful vs. Unsuccessful Conflict Resolution

Just about all of us have been in arguments that didn't go anywhere or do anything for us except make us tired and discouraged. Many couples ask themselves: "Why do we keep arguing about the same things?" Part of the answer lies in understanding the difference between successful and unsuccessful conflict resolution. The following shows these differences.

Successful Conflict Resolution

1. Problem or complaint is raised by one spouse to the other.
2. Initial attempt at solution. If none then . . .
3. Escalation into arguing.
4. Bridge building attempts by both spouses that involve:
    a. attempt to understand other's position and feelings,
    b. attempt to signal other of hope for a positive outcome,
    c. attempt to signal other of desire to maintain friendship,
    d. refusal to hit below the belt by criticizing, ridiculing, or belittling the other.
5. Problem clarification and option generation.

Unsuccessful Conflict Resolution

1. Problem or complaint is raised by one spouse to the other.
2. Initial attempt at solution. If none then . . .
3. Escalation into arguing.
4. Emotional distancing and alienation through persistent defensiveness, criticism, belittling of the other's position, and disregard for the other.
5. Further escalation of anger and hurt characterized by shouting, name calling, sometimes shoving and hitting.
6. Argument ends either by one person giving in or by two people avoiding each other. Issue is not settled, to be revisited at a later date.

Looking at the above descriptions we can see that both successful and unsuccessful conflicts start the same way but begin to deviate as the argument escalates. Successful couples engage in more bridge building behaviors and statements and are able to de-escalate the argument to the point of solving the problem. All of us want to solve problems effectively when they occur in our marriage. No one looks forward to the jagged hurt feelings that occur when we have an argument that goes nowhere. In order to maximize our ability to manage our conflicts well we need to understand a little bit about how our own personality influences the way we solve problems.

WHAT STOPS BRIDGE BUILDING?

Problems often become greater than they seem and escalate into arguments between a couple. We also know that successful spouses somehow stop the escalation and build bridges back to one another. There are three things that prevent a person from engaging in successful bridge building. They have to do with the personal issues you bring into an attempt to solve a problem.

1. Your own meta-issues and filters from your childhood:

The previous chapter on communication referred to the deeper issues and messages about ourselves that we carry around and that influence how we perceive another's communication. These meta-issues serve as filters for us and influence the way we hear another's communication. If we are sensitive about being excluded then we will listen for a threat to exclude us. If you were dominated or controlled when you were a child, either through physical or verbal abuse, then you will listen for a threat to dominate in the present moment. If you felt inadequate as a child then you will listen for any possible messages that you are inadequate now. Or you might unconsciously just want someone to take care of you and embed that message in your daily communications. Unvoiced and unmet needs can become meta-issues in your life because of your perceived inability to get them met. And most important, if your experience of anger in your family of origin was that it was toxic and threatening, you may in your present moment listen for any hint of anger in the other's voice. And you might seek to avoid the anger and just not deal with the problem.

Another difficulty with the meta-issues is that they often get communicated through the use of voice tonality and body postures, the nonverbals of communication. Thus, your spouse can ask you to shut the window, but in a way where the tone of voice communicates a demand that you perceive as dominant because your filters have you listening for dominance. And because you no longer want to be dominated like you were in childhood, you respond not to the actual request but to the perceived communication given through the voice tonality. When you respond accordingly, an argument ensues. And the two of you begin to fight on the level of your meta-issues, which represent your worst fears. All of this, of course, lies on a level just below your awareness so it is difficult to understand and stop once the argument begins.

2. The tendency to defend:

It might be part of our genetic makeup but our human psyche has equipped us with many ways to defend ourselves. This is because our egos seek to be protected from any sort of threat, real or perceived. When our spouse brings us a problem we may often respond instinctively with irritation or anger. We may begin to rationalize or blame. Or, we may just avoid the issue and not deal with it. These are usually first, instinctive responses to problems. They represent, in the best light, our need for safety and rest. We just don't want to be bothered by a problem. But your spouse might not know that and very innocently bring a problem to you. You then respond in a defensive manner, with irritation and your voice tonality communicates that irritation to your spouse. Your spouse, because of his or her own meta-issues, perceives an unresolved theme and responds accordingly. An argument escalates, not over the initial problem but over the way you responded or became defensive. And if you're not careful feelings are hurt because each of you continues to defend yourselves by blaming, being angry, and the like.

3. Stress:

It's a well-known adage in the therapy culture that when a person is under stress there is a tendency to revert to a more dysfunctional way of communicating. Not too many people, when stressed out, will communicate in a more loving and caring manner. Usually, when you're stressed, you will be more snappy, more irritable, and you will have a tendency to go back to what you learned in your own family of origin about conflict resolution. And if you learned to blame, to use anger to defend yourself when confronted, to put down, or to avoid, chances are you'll want to go back to those same behaviors. This is true even if you have decided to learn a different way to communicate. Part of this is because our brains have formed clear neural pathways for the old behaviors due to the sheer amount of repetitive behavior in childhood. So if you experienced being blamed a thousand times in childhood, the pathway of blame opens up when you're stressed and tired. And if you follow those old pathways you and your spouse can get on the escalator of harmful conflict resolution.

DEFINING THE PROBLEM

Let's assume that it's possible for the two of you to understand how your own meta-issues, tendencies to defend yourselves, and stress influence the way you communicate. Now you can go on to actually defining the problem that you need to discuss. But it's important to know what you want from the other person and when the problem will be solved. Therapists call this a well formed outcome. It's a way of asking about your immediate goals and expectations concerning problem resolution. It makes sense to have a well formed outcome, but there are many couples who simply don't take the time to really think about the problem and describe it.

Often each spouse will have a different take on what the problem is. If you give yourself time to talk about what the problem is, you maximize your chances of resolving it. However, if each of you makes assumptions about the other's point of view your attempt at problem solving can develop into a real conflict. Remember, not all problems we face need to become conflictual. Also, this process encourages the taking of individual responsibility. This process can be best described through a series of questions that you and your spouse can ask when you face conflict.

A WELL-FORMED OUTCOME: A PROCESS OF PROBLEM DEFINITION

1. First, are you aware of your own meta-issues and/or unvoiced needs? Are these in any way influencing the way you either communicate about a problem or listen to your spouse communicate about a problem? If so, take some time to surface these issues and needs and ask to speak with your spouse about them. Sometimes these issues and needs are so powerful that you might have to ask a third party to serve as a mediator/listener. This person is often a marriage therapist.

2. How do each of you define the problem? Can you describe the problem using only "I" language? Can you both agree on how the problem is defined?

3. How does this problem affect you personally, what are the consequences for you if the problem persists? For instance, are you losing sleep, worrying too much, etc.

4. If the problem involves behavior on the part of your spouse be sure to connect behaviors, feelings, and consequences. Be sure to describe only one specific behavior. Example: "When you tell me you'll be home by six and you come home at eight I feel worried and angry (feeling) because I'm not sure where you are and I can't relax (consequence).

5. How does each of you contribute to the problem? Speak only for yourselves: "my part of this problem is that I. . . ." The best way to successfully conclude an argument is for each person to talk about how he or she contributes to it and then describe how he or she can solve it.

6. Generate solutions. Again speak for yourself. What can each of you do to solve the problem? The greater the problem the greater the need to generate a solution. Generate as many solutions as possible. Spouses often limit themselves by stopping after only a few. Once you have an acceptable number of solutions begin a process of prioritizing which results in one or two solutions that you could see yourselves implementing.

Peggy and Chris have been married for fifteen years. Each was married once previously. Peggy's first marriage lasted for five years and Chris' first marriage lasted only two years. Both of them married when they were right out of high school. Neither has children from their first marriage and together they have two children ages thirteen and eleven. When they met each other they dated for two years before marrying. They both valued honesty and their friends would describe their marriage as "ideal." But the reality was a bit more sober.

Over the last few years Chris has been working longer hours and he and Peggy have gradually gotten more out of touch with each other. Then, their oldest child, Nathan, began having discipline problems in middle school. They began to argue over the right direction to take with him. Peggy would want to discuss options with Chris, but he would sometimes shut down and not want to deal with the problems. Peggy would then become quite angry with his avoidant behavior.

Peggy's world was shattered just recently when Chris confided in her that he had developed an office romance with a coworker. It had not yet become sexual but Chris conceded that it could if he let it. He had decided to be honest with Peggy since he had become more uncomfortable with the secret. Peggy was devastated since her first marriage had ended because of an affair. She had always told herself that she would not let herself be a victim to another affair. And here was Chris telling her about the office relationship and that he wanted to try to work things out. She was angry and hurt by Chris' action and wasn't sure which way to turn. In many ways she felt abandoned by Chris yet understood that he wanted to address the problem and work on the relationship. Part of her wanted to work on things; another part of her wanted to tear into him for making things so bad.

"If you're not part of the solution, you're part of the problem." Does this saying hold true for your own marital conflicts? Building bridges toward the other, especially in times of conflict, can be one of the hardest things done by a man or woman. It's natural that we want others to take our side and sympathize with our position. But when the person you look to for support is fighting with you this can become a very difficult task.

- How successful do you think you and your spouse are at building bridges toward one another in times of conflict?

- Does conflict scare you? If so, can you identify what your fears are concerning conflict?

- How can your spouse help make conflict more safe?

- In the above slice of life Peggy and Chris were unable to resolve conflict over how to handle their oldest child, and things seemed to get worse for them. If you were giving them advice what would you tell them to do differently?

THE SPIRITUAL DIMENSION: CONFLICT CAN BE HOLY

Most of us fear conflict and seek to minimize its effects on us. Yet one of the twentieth century's leading figures, Martin Luther King, Jr., used the phrase "creative tension" to describe how people who are engaged in conflict can work toward solutions. His way was the way of non-violent protest based on respect for the dignity of all people, especially those oppressed by an unjust system and by poverty.

When we are in conflict with someone we begin to feel tension, sometimes great tension. What can make the tension creative is our willingness to honor and respect the other even when we are angry, to not belittle, put down, treat poorly, or trample on his or her rights. "Creative tension" means adopting the view that the God force resides in the deepest parts of the other, and that by dishonoring the other we are dishonoring God and ourselves. "Creative tension" also encourages us to work toward a situation where both parties are winners. It means standing our ground when necessary, but in all things honoring the other as a child of God.

9

KNOW YOUR APPROACH TO CONFLICT

*I suspect that in every good marriage there
are times when love seems to fail.*

—MADELEINE L'ENGLE

The successful resolution of conflict is so important in a marriage. That is why it is important for spouses to understand how each of them enters into and resolves conflict. Each of us has a definite style in the way we approach conflict and what we do when conflict begins.

Each of us has two reactions or approaches to conflict. The first approach is our initial instinctual response, where we follow the roles and patterns that we have integrated into our personality. The second reaction or approach is how we react once conflict has escalated to a "decision point." This "decision point" is like a fork in the road. One fork takes the couple down the road where conflict continues to escalate in unhealthy ways. The other fork leads to attempts to de-escalate the conflict by building bridges and problem solving.

OUR INSTINCTUAL RESPONSE

In the previous chapter you read about the importance of problem solving as well as the larger meta-issues that sometimes prevent you from solving your problems. These are issues that are usually rooted in our own families of origin. Another thing we have learned from our families of origin is our response to conflict. We continue to use this approach because it has been, to some extent, helpful to us in negotiating conflict.

The following represent four major styles that we bring into any initial conflict.

1. Pleaser-Soother

The pleaser-soother, when faced with the initial conflict, will immediately try to make his or her spouse happy. This person's main objective is to calm down irritated feelings and try to please the other by either being agreeable or stating such things as "it's not that bad." In this person's world there is a belief that conflict is dangerous and that it can only lead to worse things happening. Further, this person believes that harmony, above all else, is the most important thing in a relationship.

This style of approach can anger the other spouse because he or she might feel that the initial approach of soothing and pleasing is in fact avoiding the problem. If you're married to a pleaser-soother try to realize that your spouse is not necessarily trying to avoid the problem as much as minimize its emotional effect. Ask your spouse to realize the importance of the problem and remind him or her that the best way of pleasing you is to address the issue directly. The positive aspect to being a pleaser-soother is that this person seeks to build the unity of the group by coming through for others. But if the pleaser-soother gets locked into this role he or she may easily become an avoider, especially if family tension and conflict are high.

2. Truth-Teller

The truth-teller is a person who is usually going to tell it "like it is," even if it might sound hurtful. This person does not hold back in terms of opinions and feelings. This person's main objective is to face whatever difficulty is confronting the marriage and to deal with it directly. The truth-teller believes that conflict is not bad, even though it may be unpleasant. The worst thing that can happen for this person is to avoid the problem and not deal with it. A truth-teller who is married to a pleaser-soother will often feel frustrated by his or her spouse's approach to conflict, and can easily label it as avoiding. The pleaser-smoother can easily see his or her spouse as too critical and judgmental. If you're married to a truth-teller the best approach is the direct one: explain your own style concerning conflict. You may also need to commit to directly saying what you want out of a specific situation.

The truth-teller brings much to any relationship because honesty can cut through to what is really going on and it can bring people to deal with hidden or unconscious issues. The negative side to being a truth-teller shows itself in the frustration that occurs when one's position or feelings are being ignored. At this point the truth-teller can become strident, feeling like the "bad guy" all the time.

3. Delayer-Avoider

The delayer-avoider is a person who clearly does not want to deal with conflict head-on. This person has learned that if you wait long enough, many problems either go away or solve themselves. This person also believes that conflict has many toxic side effects, like yelling, name calling, sarcasm, belittling, and hitting below the belt. The delayer-avoider has seen mostly the negatives of conflict in his or her own family of origin. As such, this person will spend a good deal of time waiting out conflictual times. This often angers the other spouse, especially if there is a feeling that the conflicts never get dealt with. If you're married to a delayer-avoider it's best to realize that somewhere along the line this person was harmed by the way conflict was handled in his or her family of origin, to the point of just not wanting to deal with problems. If you are a delayer-avoider you might be afraid of arguing with your spouse for fear of using the toxic communications that you learned as a child. The best thing here is to talk to your spouse about what is going on with you internally when there is an argument. If you have experienced significant emotional damage, it might be helpful for you to explore some counseling with your spouse so that you can together change the pattern.

4. Lawyer-Debater

The lawyer-debater's first approach to conflict is to take the defense position. He or she may even interrupt the other spouse's early description of the problem and begin to embark on a vigorous defense. And when the lawyer-debater has a problem it is common to ask questions as if a trial is underway. "Why did you do this at such and such a time," or "Why do you say that about me. It isn't true and I'll show you why." The lawyer-debater believes that conflict means you can't let people push you around. If you do, they will trample all over you. In this view the best defense is a good offense. This person doesn't avoid a fight, but will come out swinging when conflict begins. If you're a lawyer-debater realize that this is a style that you learned in order to defend yourself against what you thought were either superior or potentially overwhelming forces. Realize that your spouse is not one of these forces and that you don't have to protect yourself this way. If you're married to a lawyer-debater try to signal your spouse that you're not trying to prove him or her wrong, that all you want to do is to talk about a problem. Talk first about how you contribute to the problem and then ask your partner to address the problem from his or her perspective.

WHEN CONFLICT ESCALATES

Remember the model of successful conflict resolution in the previous chapter? There comes a point where we face the choice between building a bridge back to our spouse or continuing a process of harmful communication. When conflict starts a couple first attempts to solve it. Once an argument starts there are two choices: resolution or escalation. Escalation occurs when one spouse feels either that they're not being listened to, that their significant other is avoiding the problem all together, or that they're being attacked by their partner. Many arguments escalate not because people want to avoid, ignore, or attack each other; they escalate because we often mis-read each other. Also, each of the above styles has a built in "escalator," meaning that each style is capable of being interpreted negatively by the other.

Once a conflict escalates we can revert to more negative and damaging roles or we can make a choice to adopt a more positive and community building role. The following roles address both the negative and positive styles that a couple can choose to adopt when conflict escalates. I use the word "choose" quite consciously since most couples, when they escalate, fall into negative roles quite unconsciously. If you make it a point to consciously choose the role you will play when conflict escalates, you will be much more successful at resolving it.

1. The Complainer-Critic

In this role you feel that all you are doing is complaining about what is wrong. You use phrases like "you always . . ." and "you never . . ." to describe the other's behavior: "You always forget to take the trash out." At the same time your level of frustration is high because you believe that most of the time you are not being listened to.

2. The Cynic

In this role you constantly make sarcastic comments about almost anything your spouse says as the conflict escalates. You may even belittle your spouse's attempts to send a peace signal to you.

3. The Punishing Parent

In this role you first scold your spouse and then when he or she doesn't respond positively, you cut off of your spouse emotionally. You refuse to talk and refuse to consider a request to reconcile. This might go on for days.

4. The Pouting Child

It's hard to have a punishing parent without a pouting child. In this role you sulk for hours or even days, especially when your spouse clearly admits to being wrong after the argument is finished. And at the first sign of renewed conflict you retreat back into this role.

5. The Rage Warrior-Exploder

In this role you let your "anger be your guide" once conflict escalates. You explode, rant, and rave. People in your family may even be a bit afraid of your temper. And you might even feel that the explosive anger was justified by the perceived injustice done to you.

6. The Interrupter

This is the person who will interrupt his or her spouse when conflict escalates, breaking in after only a few words are spoken. Interrupting someone when conflict is escalating is a good way to ensure that conflict continues to escalate.

7. The Pursuer

When conflict escalates this person hates to be ignored and will pursue the other person into different rooms in order to make a point.

8. The Escaper

The escaper basically shuts down emotionally and withdraws physically when conflict escalates. He or she may stay in this mode for days and is usually sensitive to threat or afraid of anger.

Alternative Positive Roles

Your arguments do not have to go the direction of harmful communication and negative roles. If you discover that either of you adopts any of the above negative roles during conflict, the best thing is to talk about it when things calm down. Say what you want from each other when the conflict escalates. Commit to take a time out when you perceive you are becoming locked into a negative role. Then, consciously try to adopt one of the positive roles below. Remember, you have a choice about how you will act. Resolution may seem like the obvious choice, but it takes a lot of work. Negative roles are probably more instinctive to us when conflict begins to escalate. The following roles, when chosen, will allow each of you to feel more loved and respected.

1. Problem-Definer

In this role you define the problem as specifically as you can. You speak for yourself concerning how the problem affects you, using "I" language as much as possible. You connect events with feelings and with the impact they had on you. You also say what you want to see happen and you indicate that you're open to negotiation. "When such and such occurred I felt this way, and as a result this happened. I want the problem to be solved in this way. . . . What do you think?"

2. Bridge-Builder

Adopting this role means that you might say things like this to your spouse when conflict escalates: "I really want to be your friend and resolve this. How can we do this?" It might also mean that you take the other's side for a while in order to signal your positive attempt. "Let me get into your skin so I can understand the problem from your perspective."

3. Feeling-Affirmer

In this role you concentrate on attending to your spouse's feelings so that you do not minimize the impact of the problem. This role requires you to respond first of the other's feelings before you make your own feeling response. This requires a good deal of discipline and self-presence in order to attend to another's feelings, especially when your own feelings might be all in a jumble.

4. Content Validator-Listener

It helps when someone just hears us out and truly listens to what the other is saying without interruption. Truly indicating that you have heard the other person de-escalates the situation and helps the other find an anchor in safety and calm. Saying, "Tell me what is making you so angry," and then really listening can go a long way to resolving conflict.

5. Option Generator

This person realizes that the more options available when facing a problem, the better both spouses will feel. He or she attempts to see as many options as possible once the problem is adequately defined.

A Final Word About Anger

Anger is one of those feelings that has an especially strong impact on people. Perhaps in our own family history anger was used to protect us from danger. A father or mother might have spoken harshly to children in an attempt to protect them from danger. Whatever the case, anger seems to get our attention like no other feeling can. It's not neutral and neither is our response to anger. There are three ways to express anger: direct and congruent, indirect and passive, and aggressive.

Aggressive anger is never helpful in a marriage relationship where two spouses expect to be equals to one another and to have a relationship based on trust and safety. Aggressive anger harms the equality of the relationship and destroys the safety of the marital bond. There is always an implicit threat to use this type of anger against another person. This is why it's controlling, because people will modify their behavior because they are afraid of the other's anger.

Aggressive anger can be divided into physically aggressive and emotionally aggressive anger. *Physically aggressive anger* shows itself in physical threats, physical intimidation with one's body, throwing of objects, punching walls, pushing, shoving, and hitting.

Emotionally aggressive anger shows itself in direct insults, name calling, put downs, criticism, sarcasm, interrogating, shouting, and yelling. There is an obvious link between physically aggressive anger and emotionally aggressive anger in that emotional aggression is almost always present in domestic violence. But there are a high percentage of people who engage in emotionally aggressive anger who don't become physically violent. This type of anger is really about power and control, where one person uses anger to maintain dominance over the other.

Indirect and passive anger is often expressed through teasing, sarcasm, dirty looks, scowls, cynical comments, and the like. This type of anger is more common between married people; we act out our anger rather than talk about it. If asked to do something, we'll do it, but slowly so as to anger our spouse. If we get chewed out by a superior at work we might chew out our spouse or a child instead of directly talking about how we feel about getting a reprimand.

While it might be more common, this type of anger, over time, can also harm the relationship, slowly eroding the foundation of trust, safety, and mutual respect. A couple who wants to maximize their own marital potential would do well to consider whether this type of anger is present in their relationship. While this type of anger is also about gaining power and control, both spouses often feel that they cannot win the struggle. Still they continue to take shots at each other. It's a skirmish that cannot be won. A couple can be cynical and sarcastic with each other, and even take pot shots at each other; yet they do not fear that the anger will escalate to the point where one spouse is fearful of the other.

Direct and Congruent Anger seeks to connect events with feelings and describes the impact on the person without blaming, criticizing, becoming cynical, shouting, etc. This type of anger allows anger to be a feeling rather than a justification for retaliation. It's congruent because a person seeks to clearly express what he or she is feeling on the inside and connect it with what is happening in the external world. Also, this form of anger is directed toward very specific events and doesn't implicate the entire person. There is a big difference between hearing, "You're so stupid for doing such and such," and "When you did such and such I became angry because it caused me to be late for work." A couple that consistently strives for the direct and congruent expression of anger will maximize the potential for a successful marriage.

Take Responsibility for Your Anger. Sometimes the way you get angry is a problem in itself and requires special attention. A major criteria for seeking the help of a individual or marriage counselor should be:

- if you and your spouse have been stuck in the same pattern of escalating conflict and anger for some time;
- if the way you get angry keeps your spouse or your children from approaching you the majority of the time; all they do is to try to appease you and turn down your "anger thermostat";
- if people in your household are afraid that you cannot control your anger and you have become physically angry in the past.

If any of these are present in your relationship consider getting help by utilizing the services of a trained and qualified counselor.

In the beginning, before children, Laura found it easy to talk to her husband Frank about problems in their relationship. He was usually easygoing and able to understand her feelings on most matters. He was also quick to make suggestions and take responsibility by really listening to her suggestions.

Now, with three children ages ten, seven, and five Laura found married life to be much more complicated. They were both extremely busy and their children demanded much of their attention. They had little time for each other, and in the time they had Laura found herself bringing to Frank more and more problems. She became aware of this when Frank snapped at her one day, "Now what's the problem!"

Their arguing had increased as well. Both had a negative side to the way they engaged each other. After the argument started Laura would scold and tell Frank what his problem was. Frank would become cynical and eventually blow up at his wife, telling her that he couldn't take this anymore. Laura would then withdraw and not talk to Frank for two to three days.

On the days when there was less stress they were able to get along with each other and even enjoy the other's company. It was during these times that they talked about the patterns they had gotten into and how they wanted to change the negative way they related when tension increased. Frank could identify that he didn't like being scolded and Laura was able to tell him she didn't like his criticism and anger when they fought. Both indicated a desire to change but were not quite sure what to do differently. Both feared a repeat of the same old patterns. They both agreed to try to refrain from escalating the argument. One new thing they came up with was that each of them could call a time out during an argument as long as that person agreed to come back and finish the discussion. Both were hopeful that they could change their negative pattern but both were also a bit afraid that they were stuck in a negative conflict cycle.

Awareness in Action

When we feel pushed into a corner, or when we're under a lot of stress, it seems that there is a tendency to fight dirty or to "rant and rave." Sometimes we just get into an irritable zone where the slightest comment from our spouse elicits a negative reaction.

- Does the above slice of life appear at all familiar to you? What is your own pattern of conflict resolution?

- What positive things do you do to resolve conflict? What negative patterns do each of you bring to an argument?

- Do you see any of the above negative roles in either of your conflict resolution styles? Do you see any of the positives?

- If you decided to act differently concerning the way you handled conflict how would you be different? For instance would you take a time out, or talk about your feelings? Try to describe in specific terms what you want to work on.

THE SPIRITUAL DIMENSION:
CREATIVE TENSION

It was Martin Luther King, Jr., who used the phrase "creative tension" to describe the goals of his nonviolent approach to racial tension. His approach was rooted in respect for all people regardless of their sex or race and in taking a clear, firm nonviolent stand against injustice. His idea of "creative tension" and nonviolence was founded on a deep spirituality. He believed that through this process those who were in power would have to acknowledge those who were the victims of injustice. His approach is credited with changing the views of American society in the 1960s regarding race relations.

It's possible for a marriage to embody the spiritual principles of "creative tension" when a couple has conflicts. A creative resolution of marital problems is also founded on the absolute respect for the other person and a commitment to resolve arguments nonviolently.

This means avoiding the language of put downs, sarcasm, criticism and the many other ways we hit below the belt. It sometimes means living with a problem where there is no immediate solution. Most importantly, it means a true sharing of power between the two spouses, where there is an acknowledgment that neither one wishes to overpower or control the other. This, of course, takes a lot of "blood, sweat and tears"—as well as prayer—to make happen. But it is worth the effort.

10

CLARIFY YOUR EXPECTATIONS

Don't marry a man to reform him—
that's what reform schools are for.

—MAE WEST

To accomplish anything well we need great expectations. Expectations are created by our imaginations, they represent the outcome we are hoping for. The Olympic athlete imagines herself performing flawlessly, thus creating a positive self-expectation for the event. Without expectations we could not anticipate the future, and if our expectations are low, the future will look very bleak.

This chapter explores how we can talk about and create appropriate expectations. Before you were married you were probably told by many people that you had unrealistic expectations concerning marriage. Others told you, perhaps, that you should lower your expectation, as if marriage was an oversold commodity that wasn't worth the price. Now that you've been married for a while you have probably discovered the problem with low expectations: if you don't expect much you won't get much. Lowering your expectations only encourages you to expect less out of your marriage.

Instead, why not put the emphasis on adjusting your expectations to meet the reality of your own lived situation. This includes your own personal expectations of yourself, your work, your children, and the expectations you have of each other. Adjusting expectations involves *checking in* with each other and *checking out* your expectations. It involves some dialog and conversation.

Let's examine seven areas where married people can get themselves stuck and experience problems. Difficulties in these areas can bog you down and make you question the quality of your marriage.

1. Expectations About Your Relationship

Some common expectations go like this: As a married couple we'll be best friends. We'll do everything together. We will share our innermost thoughts. There will be no secrets. We won't get bored with each other.

When our expectations aren't met, we sometimes say to our spouse: "I thought you were my friend but . . . we're not spending much time together, we're not sharing deeply anymore, and we're fighting more." The reality of marriage often calls us to adjust our expectations. Friendships get strained and pulled in many directions. And you have all that stress to contend with: your job, your kids and their busy schedules, not to mention any unexpected developments like a health emergency.

2. Expectations About Being Lovers

Here we think: We'll make love frequently and passionately. We will be spontaneous. We will agree on the frequency of sex. We won't refuse each other. Because we are spontaneous we won't have to plan to make love.

When our expectations meet the reality of life we might think or say to our spouse: We used to be so passionate in our lovemaking, but now we don't connect with each other sexually like we used to. I wonder if you love me like you used to.

The reality of married life—especially when children come—can challenge the spontaneity and passion of lovemaking. But it doesn't mean that you have to continually lower your expectations. It means that you have to talk to one another respectfully about your expectations and needs. A complicating factor here is that you need to realize that the two of you respond to stress and tension differently. Women tend to want to be emotionally connected with their spouses before lovemaking. If there is a lot of stress then this could make it more difficult for the two of you to connect sexually. This is especially true if there is tension. For many women talking about problems with their spouse precedes lovemaking because they feel more emotionally connected. Men sometimes find it easier to put tension aside and make love to their wives. This can create confusion with women because they see their men putting off talking about tension in the relationship in favor of lovemaking. This can lead to a sense of being used. Many men see lovemaking as a way of becoming emotionally connected; this is often the opposite response to how women see lovemaking.

3. Expectations Concerning Roles and Responsibilities

Another source of tension between a couple has to do with expectations concerning roles and responsibilities. The peril of not clarifying roles and responsibilities in a marriage can certainly lead you to feel that you are stuck in a role you would rather change.

As a married couple you are partners in time. Your roles and responsibilities will shift and change as you go through transitions together. When there is tension over who does what, when, and the amount of time spent together, you might say to your spouse, "I thought we had a deal about household chores, but now I'm finding that I'm doing most of what you agreed to do and I'm feeling taken advantage of." Perhaps the general agreement you had in your early marriage has begun to break down as your children have come along. It's best to remember that every major transition will require some checking in with each other and renegotiating of the issues involved. You may still arrive at the same conclusions but now they are the result of checking in with each other and clarifying your positions. Otherwise, resentment can begin to build.

4. Expectations About Parenting

Parenting can bring out both the best and the worst in us. When we parent well, we get in touch with the loving nurturing side of ourselves. But we sometimes encounter habits and tendencies about ourselves that we didn't know were present. For instance, as your children grow older, you might find yourself being short and impatient, something you never expected. Then there is the issue of how to share parenting tasks, who does what for the children: gives them their baths, feeds them, shops for them, spends time with them.

Resentment can arise if one of you feels that the parenting load is unequally shared or if there are disagreements in how to communicate with and discipline children. Another typical pattern that causes tension has one parent—usually the husband—playing the role of the playful funny clown with the children while the other spouse is the disciplinarian and rule enforcer.

5. Happiness Expectations

Happiness expectations build on relationship and role expectations. Certainly if there are unresolved tensions in these two areas, your happiness will be lessened. But this area also has to do with your own specific happiness. Do you enjoy what you are doing, whether you are working outside the home or inside? What gives you satisfaction? What are your expectations concerning careers? Included in this set of expectations are both of your expectations about how to make decisions concerning a career path. This can be quite tricky, especially if there are hidden or unvoiced expectations about who will sacrifice for the other.

We all have a lot to be concerned about and sometimes we look to our spouse to take away our worries. Job change, loss, major illness, death of a family member, or a move to another geographical area are just a few examples of the stressful things that can happen to us. Even the birth of children, while a happy event, can create tough times for a couple and result in a change in sleep patterns, schedules, and the like.

When our expectations about how the other should be there for us aren't met we may say something like this: You said you would hang in there with me but I feel alone and abandoned. You said you would help out, but I'm carrying all the load. We want our spouses generally to "be there for us" and get hurt when this doesn't happen. Sometimes, however, we fail to adequately check out these expectations with our spouse. Remember, in times of high stress and pain it's instinctive to retreat into ourselves, to develop unrealistic expectations about how the other can care for us.

Most important, however, is the belief about happiness. Many married people believe that it is their job to make the other person happy. If you have this belief it will eventually cause you grief and bewilderment, because you cannot make your spouse happy unless he or she makes a choice to move into a higher state of satisfaction or happiness. Your job in your marriage is to listen to what makes your spouse happy and then decide if you can help him or her attain happiness. Changing your belief about happiness allows you to place the responsibility for stating what makes you happy on your shoulders as opposed to your spouse's. This means, among other things, that you will need to tell your spouse how you feel, what really interests you. It also means that you will need to really listen to what your spouse tells you about his or her happiness.

6. Expectations About Conflict

Another area of expectations has to do with how we handle conflict. As we noted in the last chapter, many of us are afraid of conflict and would just rather not deal with it. Even if we say we will face conflict with our spouse we often have unconscious, gut level responses that make it hard to do what we say we will do. So it's possible that one or both of you, even though you have verbally promised not to avoid conflict, puts off dealing with difficult things with your spouse. If this is happening the tension in your relationship will begin to escalate. It's a paradox that the avoiding of conflict actually increases marital conflict over time.

Many people believe that conflict is toxic and dangerous. If you believe this you'll probably try to avoid conflict because you expect it to damage you and the relationship. The most important thing here is for the two of you to examine your beliefs and responses to conflict so that you can resolve conflict more successfully. The most damaging thing you can do is to get into a consistent pattern of avoiding conflict with your spouse.

7. Expectations Concerning Money and Finance

Financial trouble in a marriage can be highly stressful. Marriage and family life involve many financial responsibilities, and each of you brings a set of beliefs about saving and spending money to your marriage. One of you might be a "saver," the other a "spender." One of you might want to make "safe" financial investments while the other wants to take more risks. Money, and the lack of it, has a way of defining our priorities. Chances are that both of you have some differences regarding money and you have both had to compromise. Perhaps each of you has learned something from the other regarding finances and spending. The most important thing is to recognize and discuss your areas of agreement as well as difference.

STRATEGIES TO CLARIFY EXPECTATIONS

Unclear expectations can create a good deal of conflict in a marriage. Since the two of you know each other well, it's always a good rule to surface your expectations and to talk about them when you can. The following are a few suggestions for doing just that.

1. Make the unconscious conscious. Listen to what is going on in your gut, your instinct. If something feels out of balance then share that with your spouse in a way that is respectful.

2. Check in with each other and check out your mutual expectations. Name what you want or expect in the areas of friendship, emotional support, household chores, sexual intimacy, and parenting. Listen to your spouse's needs.

3. Be ready to clarify expectations during times of transition. Also, be ready to renegotiate specific role expectations.

4. Don't ignore resentment. When you begin to feel resentment this is a sign that something is out of balance. Commit to facing this with your spouse. Don't avoid, but talk respectfully about what is going on.

5. Take responsibility for your behavior. Sometimes a previously unseen aspect of your personality will be displayed to your spouse. For instance, you may not have had a problem with anger, but now you do. Are you prepared to explore if any of this is caused by unresolved family of origin issues?

6. Work together on parenting. If your expectations differ consider taking a parenting class at your local church or school so that both of you create common expectations.

7. Clarify and talk to your spouse about your own personal happiness. Share your expectations concerning your career, how you see yourself, and if you are happy with yourself. Be ready to change your belief if you think it's your job to make your spouse happy. Be ready to talk with your spouse about what makes you happy and what you want out of life.

8. Examine your belief about conflict. Talk about whether conflict scares you and whether you avoid conflict. Above all, commit to facing conflict with your spouse. If there is something about the way you work through conflict together that you find disrespectful or not helpful, talk about it. Agree to seek professional help if the two of you cannot fix this yourself. Your relationship is worth it.

A Slice of Life

Tony and Jennifer have been married for ten years. Tony is the youngest of three children and he came from a family where his father was a perfectionist and held the children to very high standards. Growing up Tony was afraid of his father's anger, especially when he didn't achieve according to his father's standards. Tony learned at an early age that sometimes it was easier for him to fudge a bit on the truth. He found out that he could avoid his father's wrath if he stretched the truth a bit or just out and out lied to him.

This pattern of stretching the truth and sometimes lying stayed with Tony through his high school and college days. When he met Jennifer he was attracted to her energy and forthrightness. Their marriage was happy, but there was one thing that he didn't tell Jennifer, one crucial fact about himself: he didn't really graduate from college. He was three credit hours short and decided to "walk" through graduation exercises, telling his friends and family that he in fact had graduated. And he later forgot about making up the three credits.

When his employer found out that he never got a degree, they threatened to fire him for misrepresenting his background. With his work world crashing down on him he decided to confide in Jennifer. "I was afraid if you knew the truth you would get mad at me and criticize me," Tony told Jennifer. This was news to Jennifer, who only wanted to understand better why her husband didn't trust her to know the truth. After talking about this Jennifer realized that Tony brought a sensitivity to criticism into his marriage along with a fear of conflict. Tony reassured her that he would be truthful from then on. For her part Jennifer was reassured to a degree, but worried that the same pattern would reassert itself later on in their marriage.

Expectations, when left unstated, can create a great deal of tension in your relationship. Sometimes we even expect the other to know what we are thinking or feeling and get angry when our spouse doesn't respond the way we want.

- Do the two of you ever engage in a process of mind reading?

- How easy is it for you to say what you want or how you feel? Were you allowed to have a voice concerning your feelings, thoughts, and expectations when you were growing up?

- What expectations have you had to adjust since you have been married?

- In the above case Tony tried to keep the peace no matter what the consequences were for him. Have you ever become stuck or troubled because of a belief that it was your job to make people happy?

- Do you agree that clarifying your own expectations with your spouse could improve your relationship?

THE SPIRITUAL DIMENSION:
HAPPINESS AND SATISFACTION EXPECTATIONS

Does God want you to be happy in your marriage? At first glance that's an easy answer. Of course God wants you to be happy. But what's the balance between achieving your own personal happiness and your spouse's personal happiness? Sometimes your interests and expectations collide and there is conflict between the two of you. And you may even compete to get your needs and expectations met, and get angry with the other for placing his/her needs and expectations over yours.

And what makes you happy anyway? Is it in getting stuff for yourself, giving stuff (and money) away, achieving your own personal goals, helping others reach their potential? Maybe we're really the happiest when there is a balance between self-fulfillment and encouragement of the other to self-fulfillment; a balance between self-fulfillment and self-sacrifice; a balance between having for ourselves and being present to another's own developing potential. The prayer of St. Francis says, "It is in giving that we receive." Achieving this balance requires some reflection, discernment, and dialog between the two of you. And it's in that dialog that you find the presence of God.

11

RECOGNIZE PATTERNS
OF BEHAVIOR AND
<u>FACE YOUR FEARS</u>

In marriage, one can't do anything alone,
not even suffer.

—MARY ADAMS

The story is told in the Gospel of Luke about a possessed man who left his family to reside in the local cemetery (Lk 8:26-39). As Luke tells it, the man is so tormented by demons that the townsfolk resort to chaining him to the tombstones. But under the torment the man would break free of his bonds.

Then Jesus the master healer expels the demons and restores the man to complete health. Once cured, the man wants to follow Jesus and become a disciple. Jesus allows him to become a disciple but sends the man back to his family to share with his friends and family the story of his possession and healing by Jesus.

Demons can come in all shapes and sizes. As children we are taught to believe that demons actually exist in physical form, but as adults we know that the most dangerous demons are the ones we imagine. In this figurative use of the word demon we are talking about the times in our lives when we become obsessed with an idea or become compulsive about a habit that begins to eventually control us and damage our relationships. These "demons" often take the form of *things we fear* the most. And sometimes the things we fear the most influence the quality of our lives and our relationships.

Sometimes like the man in the story, we are tormented by forces that we believe to be beyond our control. Sometimes the way we behave under the influence of these forces causes us to isolate ourselves from our family and friends. It is telling that at the end of the story, Jesus sends the man back to his own family, even though he asks to become a disciple. Jesus' healing of this man in some sense involves reconciliation with the man's family of origin. All of us have unresolved issues with our families of origin that ask to be resolved one way or the other, and they often manifest themselves in the form of fears and anxieties.

PATTERNS OF BEHAVIOR

Have you ever wondered how you developed into who you are, a complex mix of emotions and personality traits? Psychologists tell us that many of these traits develop at a very early age when we are bonding with our parents or other significant adults. At this early stage of our lives we have a deep need for reassurance, nurturing, safety, and emotional contact. If a parent is physically absent or emotionally distant the child will find a number of ways to respond to the anxiety this creates. These responses eventually become patterns of behavior, or in the language of one school of psychology, "patterns of attachment." These patterns apply not only to our relationships with our parents, but to other relationships as well.

Most of us come into our adult years with a combination of healthy and unhealthy attachment patterns. When we marry, we tend to carry these patterns over to our relationships with our spouses. They are usually driven by either a need for our spouse to be closer to us or by a sense of being smothered.

Let's examine some of the more common patterns that shape our way of relating to our spouse, some of which can develop without our full awareness:

1. Angry Withdrawal

People who get caught up in this pattern often feel hurt and anger without understanding why. It may be because they feel their spouse isn't present enough. Or it may be because they are looking for approval from their spouse whom they think is withholding approval and/or affection. This sense on one spouse's part can sometimes initiate a cycle in which the other spouse also responds with anger and withdrawal.

2. Compulsive Caregiving

In this pattern one spouse consistently places the needs of the other spouse before his or her own. This pattern emerges from the belief that being a caretaker will motivate the other person to provide the level of emotional contact desired. Someone caught up in this pattern will exhibit a great deal of sensitivity to the partner and a good deal of anxiety that the other person will not be happy. One's sense of self-worth is derived from doing things for and making sure that other is happy. In marriage, this pattern translates into not being able to say no to one's spouse for fear of losing approval and valida-tion. It can lead to an even higher level of personal anxiety when one's partner is unhappy, stressed out, or angry.

3. Compulsive Self-Reliance

This pattern is the opposite of compulsive caregiving. Here there is a sense that one's needs are met best if one spouse doesn't depend on the other. There might have been an early disappointment in life where the person felt the acute absence of a caregiver and decided to face things alone. Or perhaps the family life was so chaotic that the child simply had to fend for him or herself. Whatever the case, this pattern suggests that too much closeness can be dangerous and that one needs to hide one's anxieties and protect them from discovery. Thus, to the observer, this person will appear quite self-reliant, perhaps even charming, but always in control. It is difficult for this person to form close relationships and show one's deeper insecurities to a spouse. It's not uncommon for a person who has the compulsive caregiving pattern to marry someone who has the compulsive self-reliance pattern, for the profile of self-reliance drives the fears of the caregiver that affection will one day be completely withdrawn.

4. Compulsive Care-Seeking

This pattern is characterized by a dependence on one's spouse and wanting to be taken care of like a child again. There is a sense of being helpless and a greater fear and anxiety of being cut off. When this person's stress increases due to troubles at work or on the home front there is a great deal of anxiety and many requests for comfort. This "high maintenance" care can be a pattern that only emerges fully once a marriage is underway. What the compulsive care-seeking person fears most is desertion by the caregiver. There is a great fear of being left or of not being good enough. This pattern also is characterized by a chronic low self-esteem on the part of the one seeking care.

5. Appropriate Attachments

The healthy and appropriate way out of these patterns is to articulate one's needs, anxieties, and fears and to communicate them so that one's anxieties about the future and how these needs will be met can be calmed. This pattern is characterized by the maintenance of emotional balance even when one spouse is angry with the other. There is a sense of being interdependent, meaning that a person can both meet one's own needs independent of the spouse, but also show one's vulnerability by allowing another to be caring. In a marriage this pattern also has a fair amount of give and take and negotiating between the two spouses on how the needs of each will get met.

FACING OUR FEARS

Have you ever noticed that when you are afraid you have a harder time concentrating, staying on task, performing up to your potential, not to mention relaxing? Arthur Deming, the great management guru, had as one of his first principles for maximizing human potential: "drive out all fear." This is a principle that is often easier said than done.

The thing about fear is this: we have two choices when confronted by our deepest fears. We can either face them or run from them. When we face them we usually win a greater sense of self and solid identity. This is hard work. When we run from them we usually employ the psychological mechanisms of denial, rationalization and defensiveness in order to justify our decision to avoid facing our fears.

The following represent some of the deeper fears that we will face in life. Each fear is rooted in some way in one of the attachment patterns described above. With each fear you will identify an accompanying negative belief that often reinforces and sustains the cycle of fear. Finally, some suggestions will be given concerning how to face the particular fear and what you can do about it. Most of us we will identify with one or two of the deeper fears; some of us might identify with all of them.

Fear of Rejection / Abandonment

Abandonment is the other side of belonging. The belief associated with this fear says that the people the closest to you will either leave you or find you wanting. When you have this fear you don't trust that you belong to whatever group you're in. You're always looking for the first sign of trouble, the first sign that someone will show you the door. You might even misinterpret someone's body posture, a frown, what you think is a scowl or dirty look. When this happens you might say to yourself, "What did I do wrong?"

This fear can lead a person to work very hard at gaining the acceptance of others, even to the point of sacrificing personal needs. There is an inordinate "need to be liked," because when we are liked we are then accepted. Abandonment fears are common in people who have come from homes where one or both parents used emotional cut-off to control behavior. "If you don't do what I want, I won't be accessible to you" is the message behind this fear. There are some who act out of this fear in an openly anxious manner and are quite sensitive to any threat of being cut off or excluded. The person who is sensitive to being excluded might join many groups and have a difficult time saying no, for fear that their "no" will lead to rejection. This fear also leads to a deep insecurity and can cause intense jealousy.

Fear of Failure and Incompetence

Have you ever bemoaned the fact that you were just not smart enough, creative enough, or good enough to get ahead at work? Or have you felt that you don't deserve the success you already have, that one day people will discover you are a fraud impersonating a successful person? If so, then you have just named one of your fears, the fear of failure and incompetence. This fear is born out of the belief that we can gain love and acceptance through performing well. This is a very common fear in our society today, which places a high emphasis on competence and performance in work, leisure, and home life.

People who have this fear can come from very "normal" families, but there is usually the presence of perfectionism on the part of one or both of the parents. Perfectionism creates an environment where there are very high moral and educational standards. Children who are raised with a perfectionistic standard can easily develop a feeling of inadequacy, especially if they find themselves failing to meet their own expectations as well as the expectations of their parents.

There is also a good deal of anger generated by this fear, anger at oneself for not being good enough, and "sideways" anger that seeps out of the cracks and gets directed at our loved ones. Procrastination is also a big problem for people beset by this fear; because they believe that they can never do a job good enough, they put off the completion of the project. The person facing this fear somehow has learned to associate affirmation and love with performance: the better you do in sports and in school the more positive feedback you will get from us as your parents. In this family failure is simply unacceptable.

This is a fear that affects people who are establishing their careers or who have had some real experience of workplace setback or failure. Someone who has a fear of failing will have a difficult time relaxing and having fun. Being hard on oneself comes with this territory, and you might find yourself complaining more than you want; you may even then become defensive when your spouse gives you suggestions about doing better. Your spouse might even grow tired of listening to the ever present anxiety concerning failure. The other major problem that can arise out of this fear is a difficulty with the setting of limits concerning how much and long you work. Gaining affirmation through work and performance is a recipe for creating a workaholic.

Fears of Not Enough Intimacy, Too Much Intimacy

These fears can be set side by side since they arise out of the same theme of intimacy. With these fears we feel either cut off from love or overwhelmed by love. The person who feels cut off from love has an abiding sense of never being able to receive enough affirmation and acceptance and fears that he or she will live a life of loneliness. This person may become either a caretaker or a care seeker. He or she may experience a spouse as inaccessible or distant and make various attempts to communicate and become closer, only to be rebuffed and hurt. This person also may feel that the quality of friendship is lacking and may have anxiety concerning being able to form close and lasting bonds with others.

On the other side of the spectrum is the person who feels overwhelmed and smothered by attempts of others to become emotionally close. This person may have the compulsive self-reliant pattern and is used to being independent and doesn't look to others to meet many of his or her needs. This person may have a high need for a lot of alone time, and may express dissatisfaction with close associates who show their deeper emotional selves. This person may have come from a family where close emotional support was either lacking or inconsistent, and therefore learned to insulate him or herself from the lack of intimacy.

Fears of not enough intimacy or being smothered by intimacy can cause a couple to do a "dance of intimacy" where the spouse who is more "intimacy seeking" pursues the spouse who is more "intimacy fearing." When this occurs there is usually a lot of marital dissatisfaction.

Fear of Conflict

This might be the marital "mother of all fears" because a fear of conflict can prevent a couple from solving even the most basic problems that arise. Often, the person who is a care-taker or peacemaker will show a fear of conflict and sometimes an outright avoidance of it. This fear usually has its roots in a person's primary family of origin where one learned that conflict is a toxic thing to be avoided at all costs. People who are peacemakers often fear conflict. Their experience has been one of unsolved, frequent conflict, verbally and perhaps also physically abusive. A person who fears conflict in a marriage can avoid his or her spouse, especially when emotions run high over a problem.

Six Steps to Facing Fear

Unfaced fears can lead to all sorts of harmful things: addiction, inappropriate anger, an abiding feeling of insecurity, a "driven" personality, eating problems, and poor conflict resolution skills. The following might help you in identifying your fears with your spouse:

1. Name your fears

Giving voice to the unconscious fears you may have is the first place to start. Naming what is going on with you allows you to create options and exercise greater control over your life.

2. Realize that your worst fears often don't come true

When they do you have more skills than you realize to deal with them. Unfaced fears are like shadows we cast that appear larger than life. When we turn and face them and shine the light of reflection on them they almost always shrink to a size that is manageable.

3. See your spouse as your ally in facing your fears

Think about what you need from your spouse in order to talk about your fears? A listening ear? Advice? A sounding board? It's important to define your spouse's role if you're going to take on this task. Sometimes you will be confused by what you want from your spouse in this regard; hang in there and trust that your instincts will tell you what you want.

4. Deal with your anger

Don't use anger to control or to defend yourself. If you have identified yourself as having any of the attachment patterns listed above it's possible that you use your anger either to protect yourself or to express your anxiety when your stress is too high. This type of anger can be destructive, not only to you but to your relationship. This is anger as a defense, not as a feeling. It keeps people away from you. Commit to doing better with your anger, and if you need to talk to someone about it, take the risk to do better.

5. If your fear involves your spouse, commit to talking this out

Be reciprocal with each other. Can you reassure your spouse about some fear? Are you willing to face how you participate in the maintaining of the fear if it's an issue?

6. Consider getting into marriage counseling

Seek counseling with your spouse if the fear and problem become ever present and unmanageable. Early detection of marital problems is actually a sign of health. The quicker you act to solve the problem effectively the better your marriage will be.

Chad and Jennifer have been married for fifteen years. Their oldest daughter is now a freshman in high school. Just five years ago Jennifer was diagnosed with breast cancer and had a radical mastectomy, followed by radiation treatments for six weeks. After the treatments were finished she had reconstructive surgery. She has been cancer free for five years and the doctors assure her that her prognosis continues to look very good.

Since their oldest daughter became a teen Chad has noticed a gradual but clear change in Jennifer. Over the last year and a half Jennifer has gained about 20 lbs and has become more snappy to those in her family. Her relationship with her daughter has gone from good to strained. They seem to fight all the time.

What is more, Chad has also noticed that Jennifer's consumption of alcohol has gone up considerably over the last year. She used to have an occasional drink. Now she is drinking up to four glasses of wine an evening. Chad has quietly taken to marking the wine bottle in the refrigerator so as to monitor her consumption level.

When he has raised his concerns with Jennifer she has been stubborn and defensive. Jennifer describes as "ridiculous" his concerns about her drinking and becomes quite defensive when he tries to talk to her about her weight. She accuses him of being insensitive and heartless when he attempts to share his concerns. She has said to him on a number of occasions, "Take me as I am. Either love me or leave me." Those discussions usually end up in tears and Chad feeling like he is the bad guy.

Chad thinks that Jennifer has become more depressed in the last year and a half and may even be jealous of their oldest daughter moving into puberty. When he said this to Jennifer she accused him of playing "psychologist" and told him that until he had a life threatening illness he would never understand how she felt.

Their teen daughter has begun to catch on to the growing tension between the two, and even to Jennifer's increased drinking. Chad is beginning to withdraw more from Jennifer. He realizes that this can only make things worse, but he is feeling helpless about what to do. He even called Jennifer's doctor, who agreed that Jennifer might be depressed. The doctor recommended that Chad talk to Jennifer again and persuade her to address her depression. "Easier said than done" Chad said to himself after talking to the doctor.

Awareness in Action

Sometimes we become our worst enemies because of our inability to deal with our fears and anxieties. Marriage is about sharing our vulnerabilities and underdeveloped selves with our spouses. Yet sometimes we fail to do so because of embarrassment, shame, or fear of criticism. Could you, or have the two of you ever had a dialog similar to the one described above? In the case above it's possible that Jennifer has some unexamined fears associated with her cancer recovery.

- Sometimes life's troubles can rattle our sense of safety and security. Is it easy or difficult to share your vulnerabilities with your spouse?

- Do you recognize yourself in any of the attachment patterns listed above?

- Why, if we are life partners, do we sometimes not communicate our fears and worries to our spouse?

- Are there any fears in this chapter with which you identify? Are there others not listed here that occupy your time and attention? Can you share them with your spouse?

THE SPIRITUAL DIMENSION:
LETTING GO OF FEAR TO TRUST

In the Gospel of Luke the opposite of faith is not disbelief but fear. The Jesus that Luke presents seems to understand the human psyche very well. Again and again Jesus suggests to his followers that fear holds us back and that it robs us of our full potential. In the story of the calming of the sea (Lk 8:22-25) we find the disciples crossing the lake in the boat while Jesus sleeps. A storm comes upon them threatening to swamp the boat, and of course the disciples become afraid. They wake Jesus who challenges them about their faith. He then calms the storm.

Another way to look at this story is this: perhaps Jesus challenged his disciples not only to trust God, but to trust as well their own instincts and skills. After all, they had been on the lake many times before and were most likely skilled and experienced sailors.

What about you? Do you believe that God is present to your own inner instincts and skills? Do you trust that or are you afraid of believing in yourself? One of the most important shifts in adult life comes when we understand that God is "within" our experiences and instincts as much as God is external to ourselves. How would it change you if you began to trust your instincts and feelings as indications of the presence of God?

12

TAKE CARE OF YOURSELF AND YOUR SPOUSE

Do what you can, with what you have,
where you are.

—THEODORE ROOSEVELT

It might seem strange to suggest that an important strategy for insuring the success of your marriage has to do with a commitment on your part to take care of yourself over the course of your marriage. It's a fact, however, that many spouses spend more time worrying about their partners than themselves, to say nothing about the worry over children.

The other side of worry is wellness. Marriage, when it's working right, can be seen as a community of wellness, where each of you actively seeks to be well and encourages the other to seek wellness. When it comes to taking care of yourself, the following go into a comprehensive list of factors that comprise wellness. These factors, when applied to your relationship, have the potential to increase both your personal and marital satisfaction. This list is presented to you and your spouse in the hopes it will enable you to have a more comprehensive conversation about how each of you takes care of yourself. Wellness is a sense of balance and well being which comes from integrating the many diverse but interconnected parts of the self. Wellness consists of the interaction of the following parts of our lives:

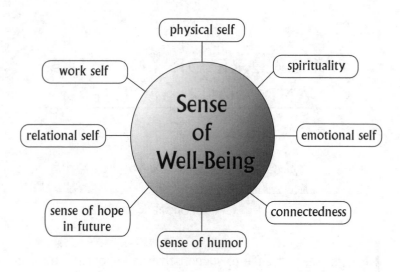

Physical Self:

This part of the self comprises our body image, how we feel about our bodies, whether we feel fit, overweight, too thin. The question here is, are you comfortable in your own skin? This sense of physical self comes to us in part from what we were taught about our bodies by our own families and in part by our own genetic heritage. Ask yourself honestly: Do you feel good about how you are taking care of your physical self? Do you get enough exercise? When under stress do you sometimes harm your body by either drinking or eating too much? Do you consume too much caffeine? What could you be doing differently to take care of yourself in this area?

Work Self:

This part of the self has to do with how you interact with others at work, whether you are happy with your work and have a sense of direction to your career. Do you feel trapped by your job, do you find yourself complaining about your work? Does your work give you energy or take energy from you? If you feel stuck what, if anything can you do differently to start feeling unstuck?

Relational Self:

This is the part of the self that has to do with how you are in relationship with the significant people in your life, your spouse, your children, co-workers, friends and other family members. Do you feel connected to these people? Is your relationship with your spouse energy-producing or energy-sapping? With your children, energy-producing or energy-sapping? What can you do to show the ones who care about you that you want to improve on the relationship you have right now with them?

Emotional Self:

This is the part of the self that has to do with how we feel about ourselves and the world on a daily basis. This part of the self is affected by our own family background, our genetic makeup and also by the amount of stress that we find ourselves under. This is also the part of ourselves that has to do with reaching out and developing friendships with others. But sometimes we are just too busy to take care of our emotional selves and we fail to recognize the signs of burnout, depression, or anxiety. Do you take the time to adequately relieve your stress in a healthy way through exercise and leisure? If you are slightly burnt out or depressed do you allow your spouse to raise this issue with you or do you get defensive and refuse to think about it? What positive steps can you take to improve upon your own mental health?

The Spiritual Self:

This addresses the part of the self that asks the bigger questions of where we came from, how did it all begin, is there a God who cares about you. This is the sense of self that struggles with the tough questions, like why do good people suffer. It's also the part of the self that sees a deeper meaning in making connections among one's various endeavors. These connections can be found through the practice of religion, but they can also be found in work with the poor, the environment, or the many other good causes that exist today. Through the spiritual sense of self one asks the deeper questions about good and evil, values and your place in the scheme of things. Do you feel connected to the larger issues? Are their organizations or causes outside your own marriage and family that draw your attention and give value and meaning to your life?

The Playful Self:

This addresses the part of the self that wants to play and relax, to unwind, to relieve stress, and to transcend the problems of life that always seem to be ready to pounce on us. Laughing releases endorphins and allows us to rejuvenate ourselves. Why do children have the capacity to laugh, cut loose, play, have fun, while we adults struggle just to enjoy a little part of our day? Children are not usually beset with all the concerns of life as you are. Do you have a laughter and leisure deficit? Are you working too long, getting less ahead, and not having any fun? Has your own life, maybe even your relationship with your spouse gone a little stale? What can you do to add some fun to your life? What can the two of you do together to have fun and enjoy your life?

Through the Years

Okay, you're probably sold on the idea of wellness. After all, who can be against wellness? But as you get older you will begin to understand that, if you want to be as healthy as possible, you need to attend to these factors. Gradually—and sometimes not too gradually—we age and there will come a time when we face the limits of life. All of us will die one day, no matter how much we follow our culture's denial of death. But do we want to face getting older in a way that emphasizes health and wellness, actively striving to take care of ourselves? Think of it this way: if we neglect our bodily and emotional well being most likely we will have more illnesses in our lives and feel more depressed about ourselves. And it's possible that as we get older we will find ourselves more limited by the impact of not taking care of ourselves. Wellness is not a way of denying the inevitability of death, it's a way of understanding ourselves as persons who realize the limit imposed by death. That's why spirituality is a big part of wellness, the limit of death forces us to ask the bigger questions concerning life after death and God.

The paradox of wellness is that you cannot force your spouse to take care of him or herself. Try as you like if your spouse refuses to watch his or her cholesterol and weight there is little you can do to force the issue. The same is true of something like smoking; you can limit smoking to only the outdoors and you can tell your spouse how unhappy you are about it but unless your spouse truly decides to quit, this will probably be a losing battle for you.

Four Vital Questions

There are four vital questions that each of us can ask our partner about health and wellness:

1. How do you feel about yourself?

This is a question we can ask frequently. How do you feel about yourself physically, emotionally, relationally? To really ask the question out of concern for the other and to really listen to their response is an act of love. How do you feel, really? This is a good question to ask of each other on a regular basis because it indicates that you really care for each other.

2. How do you take care of yourself?

This is another vital question that puts the responsibility for taking care of self on the shoulders of the individual. You are the only person who knows what it feels like to be in your skin. No one else knows that experience like you do. You know best what you need in order to take care of yourself. That is why your spouse asks how you're doing, how you're taking care of yourself. Sometimes you might want to fault your spouse for not taking care of you, and sometimes your spouse might be insensitive to your needs. But the responsibility for stating how you're to be cared for starts with you.

3. What do you want for yourself, from me?

In the areas of wellness outlined above the question of want becomes very specific. What do you want for yourself physically, emotionally, spiritually, etc? To ask this question means that your spouse really cares how you are doing emotionally, physically, spiritually, relationally. To ask this question means that the two of you might have to take some time to talk all this through. Also, in speaking of what you want for yourself you might also uncover something that you want your spouse to consider doing. If you make the request realize that it has to be delivered freely, meaning that your spouse might suggest a modification or might not be able to do what you want exactly the way you want it.

4. How can I help you take care of yourself?

While each of us has to realize that we cannot do it all, there are ways we can help. For instance, suppose that your spouse wants to quit smoking. Your question then becomes, "How can I help you? Is there anything I can do?" Asking it this way might help you avoid nagging, demanding, and criticizing if your spouse doesn't always follow through on the commitment.

A WORD ABOUT ALCOHOL AND SUBSTANCE ABUSE

How we take care of ourselves and handle the stress of life is an important decision for all of us. It's no surprise that people often turn to alcohol and other substances to help them unwind. Alcohol still remains the drug of choice for the majority of citizens in the United States. Certainly, it's okay to have a drink. Part of the problem is that ninety percent of people who become addicted to a drug are not aware that they are crossing the line from occasional use to addictive use.

What are some of the signs that you might be crossing that line? Looking forward to your next drink, drinking to relieve stress and tension, an increase in consumption, the subject of drinking becomes a source of tension at home, and a decrease in work performance due to drinking or another substance are major indicators. The key question is: Are you in control of the substance or is it in control of you? For instance, can you go out with friends or to a party and not drink at all and have fun? If not, then maybe the substance is more in control of you than you realize.

Connie and Mike have been married for nineteen years. They have two teens, ages sixteen and fourteen. Both Connie and Mike have taken relatively good care of themselves through the years, although both of them have struggled a bit with weight gain. When Connie was forty-two she entered menopause; this development caught both of them off guard. Before menopause she began having irregular menstrual cycles. As this process developed Connie experienced mood swings, hot flashes, muscle pain, and she also began to gain more weight. She knew that she was experiencing a mild form of depression as a result of this transition, especially since it came years before she was expecting.

Mike, of course, was affected by the impact of menopause and often felt helpless. He wasn't sure how to support her on questions such as estrogen replacement therapy. Mike was also concerned about Connie's depression and was worried about her weight gain, but he was reluctant to talk about this because he feared she would be defensive. Both of them struggled with the transition, each from their own perspectives.

Connie's doctor gave her permission to grieve and face the transition ahead of her. She gave Connie valuable information concerning estrogen replacement therapy and invited her and Mike to discuss together the options that Connie had. She also framed the transition in a positive light and emphasized with Connie the importance of eating well and getting regular exercise. As a result Connie began to develop a plan that included diet changes and more regular exercise. She also became more clear with Mike about how he could support her and what she needed from him as she moved through this transition.

Mike also faced his own reactions to this transition. He had not anticipated that Connie would enter menopause so early. He was in good shape, athletic and worked out regularly. During this transition he became acutely aware of how much he valued physical activity and sexual contact with Connie. He saw her struggle with mood swings, depression, and weight gain and he tried as best he could to be supportive. He was determined to be positive but was also afraid to share with her any of his own reaction for fear that she would become more depressed and defensive.

AWARENESS IN ACTION

Stress is a part of daily living, yet we sometimes desensitize ourselves to its impact on us. We work hard, sometimes very long hours. And we sometimes forget that we have all those different and good parts to ourselves.

- How well do you take care of yourself? Do you have concerns about the way your spouse takes care of him or herself? Can you discuss these concerns with your spouse in a non-defensive and caring manner?

- Are there any areas of wellness listed above where you could be doing a better job taking care of yourself?

- What action can you take to feel better about yourself?

THE SPIRITUAL DIMENSION: WHOLENESS IS HOLINESS

This phrase sums up the idea that the quest for holiness is a holistic endeavor involving all parts of the human person: the thinking, feeling, physical, psychological, and sexual parts of who we are, as well as how we were formed in our own families of origin. To be holy, to be whole, is to be well at its most fundamental level.

There is a paradox to being well, to being whole, in that in order to truly be whole we have to be open to moving through pain and brokenness toward healing. To be open to love is to be open to having our heart broken. Not allowing our hearts to take this risk means shutting ourselves off from the risk of love. This isn't being whole, it's being scared and afraid.

But to be whole means that we take the risk of love and life, and face our pain, not run from it or seek to avoid it by self-medicating with alcohol or other drugs. If you are to be a whole person you have to embrace the fragmented parts of your life; some of these parts you are sometimes not too proud of. They represent the unfinished business of your life's journey and they cry out for integration.

Being open to the God-force in your life means being open to pain, but also to healing. A man who was about to die from a terrible cancer, told a minister who visited him right before he died, "Even though I'm dying, I've been made whole." He had reached the wholeness that lies beyond pain and suffering.

13

CHANGE YOURSELF,
ACCEPT YOUR SPOUSE

After marriage, all things change. And one
of them better be you.

—ELIZABETH HAWES

In the movie *As Good As It Gets* Jack Nicholson plays a
querulous writer who suffers from obsessive compulsive
disorder (OCD). He meets a waitress played by Helen Hunt
and gradually develops a relationship with her. He quickly dis-
covers that he is attracted to her balanced, even personality
and falls in love with her. As a result of his falling in love he
decides to go back on medication to control his OCD. And at
the climax of the movie, when his relationship with her hangs
in the balance he says to her, "Knowing you has made me want
to be a better man."

This is a great summary of what marriage is all about. In the
best moments of our marriage we can say to our spouse,
"Knowing you makes me want to be a better person." The
desire to be a better person brings us to the crossroads of
change, and to take responsibility for how we want to change.

One of the toughest transitions any married person goes
through is the transition from asking your spouse to change
to accepting responsibility to change yourself. Obviously it's

easier if the other person changes. But the request for change that we make of our spouse often resides on an unconscious or semi-conscious level. We can easily fall into a power struggle with our spouse over how things are done, which habits are found distasteful, and which needs aren't met. You may even struggle with the reasons why you're having power struggles!

WE GROW ON OUR DIFFERENCES

One reason the request for change causes problems has to do with how the two of you met each other and fell in love. There is a saying in the marriage therapy field: "We meet on what we share in common, we grow on our differences." In the beginning, when you fell in love with each other, you probably experienced a large area of common feelings, values, and interests. You may even have learned new ways of doing things from each other, and new interests as well. When you look back on this period, you will probably discover a lot of good will toward sharing common interests and values. Concerning the differences you had at the time, you both were probably optimistic that you could compromise. Indeed, you may have enjoyed a good track record at resolving your differences. And it makes sense that your ability to compromise and tolerate differences should carry into your marriage. Why then are you arguing more and compromising less?

As we settle into marriage more of our hidden self emerges. It's not that we intentionally hide things from our spouse; sometimes we even hide them from ourselves. For instance, someone who comes from a family where one or both parents expressed a good deal of anger may decide to adopt a more "laid back" approach toward conflict. His or her fiancé may be attracted to this calm approach. But, as the marriage unfolds, what a surprise it is to find that this person sometimes has a difficulty with anger, just as one of his or her parents did. This "hidden" aspect to the personality emerges over time in the marriage. There are many "hidden" parts to us that can create surprise in our relationships.

Whenever a change occurs, hidden aspects of ourselves can surface. The birth of a child, a move, a job change, indeed any stressful situation can bring something previously unseen to the surface.

Another reason this happens is the very safety of marriage. Because we trust our spouse to be there and remain faithful to our marriage commitment, we feel freer to "tell things like they are." We can speak our mind more freely or do things more freely.

Nevertheless, when differences emerge in a relationship it can be a time of real tension, but also real growth. Maybe there is something built into our genetic structure that encourages us to see differences as a threat. Perhaps we secretly fear that if our spouse is truly different in some way he or she will stop loving us and leave us for someone more like them.

The crisis that a couple faces when serious differences emerge can be voiced one of two ways. The first way says, "I don't understand why you think and feel differently from me. If you were only more like me, things would be different." The second way says, "I sometimes get a bit exasperated and maybe a little afraid that we have different ways of thinking and feeling, but I want to appreciate that we're different and try to understand our differences in a way that enhances our relationship. I don't want to see differences as bad."

DEALING WITH DIFFERENCES

The following points might help you grow on your differences and negotiate the change you want in your relationship.

- There are differences in temperament that can sometimes cause problems if not understood properly. One of you might be more spontaneous, the other more structured; one of you might be a thinker, the other a feeler;

one might be more physically expressive, the other might be more reserved. Allow yourself to think of these differences in a neutral way.

- There are also differences in the way people solve conflict. One of you might be more at ease with conflict, the other might tend to avoid it. Don't spend time wishing the other would change. Rather talk about your own approach, and commit to negotiating a style that respects each of your approaches. You might have to get into marriage counseling to do this negotiating, especially if the two of you feel especially stuck.

- Give up trying to change the other. People only change and do something different when they are ready to. You are allowed to say what you want and what would make things more helpful to you, but pouting and getting angry with your spouse for not doing things your way will only make matters worse. When you give up trying to change your spouse, it begins to free your spouse to take more responsibility. This is because the two of you are not in a "push-pull" power struggle characterized by stubbornness and resistance.

- Know your own bottom line non-negotiable values like respect, honesty, trust, etc. If any of your spouse's behaviors violate these values, this is a signal to get into marriage counseling. You do not have to put up with behaviors that violate your bottom line values. For instance, if you're married to someone who abuses alcohol, you can't make your spouse stop, but you can refuse to ride in the car when she or he is drinking. And you can attend an Al-Anon group.

- On behaviors that don't violate your bottom line non-negotiable values: keep your focus on the behaviors, don't attack the person. Tell your spouse about the particular personality traits that you are striving to accept.

Ask your spouse to discuss this with you, and if you need outside help, get it.

- Take responsibility for how you want to change. This is scary. It keeps the focus on your behaviors. Your behaviors are in the circle of your control. For instance, if you're not happy with your life and have been subtly blaming your spouse for this, start thinking about what you can do to achieve greater personal happiness.
- Talk together about the changes you want to make, personally and in your relationship. Speak for yourself, not for the other. Create a plan if you can. Encourage each other, but don't demand.

BLOCKS TO CHANGE

Have you ever had the experience of attempting to change something in your life yet found that you couldn't quite get the job done? Why is it that change is sometimes so difficult? Below are four reasons why we sometimes find ourselves blocked when we face changing something about ourselves. The following represent reasons why change is so difficult. Identify the ones holding you back from making the change you want.

Fear

We're often afraid of trying something new, either because we are not confident or because of our past experiences. Fear can keep us chained to old behaviors that are unhealthy and even harmful.

Negative Self-Talk

Have you noticed how sometimes we tell ourselves we are either not good enough, not smart enough, or not attractive enough? We give ourselves hundreds of messages every day. These messages reinforce a pattern of behavior. Negative self-talk usually leads to self-defeating behaviors.

Lack of Consistent Encouragement

Child experts tell us that in order for a child to have positive self esteem it needs to hear five positive comments for every negative comment. The same ratio holds for adults.

Cost of Change Is Perceived as Too Great to Offset the Gain of Change

Every significant change involves a cost or loss and a possible gain. A person who gets married, for instance gives up the single life for the gain of marital intimacy. Another person might want to quit smoking but not want to give up the pleasure of it. In order to really change we must be convinced that the benefits will be greater than the cost.

Lack of Options

Sometimes we want to change but don't know that we can. We might feel that we are destined to remain in a state of unhappiness because we simply don't know that there are options available to us.

Complaining Is Easier Than Changing

It's a lot easier to complain about one's lot in life than to do something about it. Change takes a conscious decision and requires work on our part.

CAN YOU REALLY CHANGE?

Change can be both fearful and exhilarating, but to change we must overcome our built-in tendency toward habit. We often just do things because we're used to the pattern. Our brains form neural pathways that become reflexive. Changing the neural pattern takes time, but not as much time as you think. Below are some suggestions that might help in creating the change we want to see happen in our lives.

Know what you want.

A well-formed outcome that states the behaviors you want to change and the new behaviors you want to adopt. Example: "I want to control my temper and be more relaxed."

Change your self-talk.

We are continually giving ourselves messages about what we want, who we are, and how we feel about ourselves. Become aware of how you talk to yourself and change the negatives to positives.

Find someone who can act as a coach or mentor.

Finding the right person to give encouragement and give suggestions on specific strategies is very important. This could be your spouse, but be clear as to what you're are asking for.

Imagine yourself adopting the change you want.

See yourself completing the change. What will be different about you once you successfully adopt the change?

Identify the new behaviors that can substitute for the old behaviors.

Be as specific as you can. Many people give up because they don't get specific enough.

Create either a Personal Plan, a Relationship Plan, or a Career Plan.

State your goal or outcome, how you want to change on both the belief and behavior level, and how you are going to get there.

A Slice of Life

Scott and Cindy's marriage of fourteen years was at the point of breaking up. Scott had suddenly announced that he was leaving and told Cindy that he "couldn't take it anymore." This was a surprise to her and she pleaded with him to get into some form of marriage counseling with her.

During the marriage counseling it finally came out that Scott never liked the fact that when they argued Cindy would raise her voice and yell at him. He would become quiet at times and leave the room, only to have Cindy become more vocal and pursue him. Cindy was surprised that her yelling had such a negative effect on him. She had come from a very expressive family where verbal arguments and raised voices were just a normal part of her life.

Scott also felt that Cindy would become critical of him when he would spontaneously announce that he had plans for their weekend. At times it would seem that Cindy would resist every one of his suggestions. What Scott didn't understand was that Cindy was the type of person who wanted to plan ahead. She tended to be more organized and liked to talk about weekend plans in advance. Cindy also got frustrated and angry with Scott when he sprung activities on her. To her it seemed disrespectful. That's when the yelling began. Scott had consistently felt criticized yet he admitted to not making much of an attempt to talk to her about his negative reaction to the way they argued and the way they planned.

Both of them became aware that they spent a lot of time wishing that the other would change and that there had been a long simmering power struggle between them. They both agreed that each of them could take responsibility to change certain specific things, that Cindy could work on arguing without yelling and Scott could work on becoming more direct with Cindy about what he wanted and communicating with her more. Both also realized that there were also acceptance issues as well that each needed to work on. And both wondered if too much damage had already been inflicted on their relationship.

We are often used to getting what we want. Sometimes we take a consumer attitude toward our significant relationships and think of our spouse as a complaint department. We think to ourselves, "if only you would change or do it my way things would be so much better." In the above case Scott didn't stick up for himself and perhaps had some wishful thinking about Cindy's changing her behavior. Eventually he had to face whether it was worth him changing by speaking his mind more clearly to Cindy.

- Do you think there have been times when the two of you have fought over change and who will change?

- Does it make sense that accepting your spouse and changing yourself is the better way, even though it is more difficult?

- What, if anything, is blocking you from making the changes you want?

- Are there any negative messages you give yourself? What are they?

- Can you identify any new behaviors you want to adopt? Can you identify any new beliefs about yourself that you want to adopt?

- Who can serve as a coach and help you identify the changes you want to make?

THE SPIRITUAL DIMENSION:
A PRAYER FOR SERENITY

It is perhaps best known as the Serenity Prayer, having been adopted by twelve step groups as a common prayer which expresses the desire for change. It is also a great prayer for married couples.

> God,
> grant me serenity to accept the things I cannot change,
> the courage to change the things I can
> and the wisdom to know the difference,
> living one day at a time,
> enjoying one moment at a time,
> accepting hardship as a pathway to peace,
> taking, as Jesus did, this sinful world as it is,
> not as I would have it,
> trusting that you will make all things right
> if I surrender to your will,
> so that I may be reasonably happy in this life
> and supremely happy with you forever in the next.
>
> —REINHOLD NEIBUHR

14

KNOW YOUR
BOTTOM LINE VALUES

Who so loves,
believes the impossible.
—ELIZABETH BARRETT BROWNING

There is a biblical story about trading away one's birthright. As the story goes, Esau, the older brother, was a hunter, while Jacob "kept to his tents" (Gen 25:27). Being the first born Esau was entitled to a double share of his father Isaac's heritage. Since Jacob "kept to his tents" he had time to think, and to scheme against his brother. One day Esau returned from a hunt famished. His brother was cooking stew and Esau asked for some. But Jacob said, "First, give me your birthright in exchange for it." "Alright," said Esau, "I'm at the point of dying. What good will any birthright do me?" So he swore an oath to give Jacob his birthright. He later, of course, regretted giving away his birthright for a mere bowl of lentils.

While we may smile at this story, don't we do the same sometimes? We trade away the things that are most precious to us because we feel needy, alone, desperate, hungry, or afraid. This odd couple of Jacob and Esau is no model for marital give and take, but they do remind us that marriage is often about compromise and negotiation. While compromise is essential, it is important to realize that there are some underlying, non-negotiable values that form the foundation of your commitment to one another. And as the story shows, it is not a good idea to trade away your core values for peace and security in your marriage, or because you are afraid.

What's Negotiable, What Isn't?

It's important to understand that there are a handful values that form the bedrock of your marriage. If these values are violated the firm ground on which your foundation rests is shaken. Then your marriage is in serious trouble. This doesn't mean there's no hope, but it calls for serious attention. On the plus side, knowing what is not negotiable for you, it's possible that you will feel the freedom to understand that there is a very wide area where many things are negotiable. Here, then are four bottom line non negotiable values that form the bedrock of any mature marriage.

1. Respect

Aretha Franklin made this word famous. It is, above all else, a word that defines the quality of a relationship. There are at least three important meanings to respect. The first is to show another person high regard and esteem. The second has to do with not intruding on another's boundaries, while the third meaning is honoring of another's wishes and intentions.

To respect your spouse, then, you must demonstrate that he or she counts. High regard means that when your spouse talks you listen, that you admire his or her qualities and know that to be in your spouse's presence is a good thing for you. When you respect your spouse, you sometimes even brag about him or her. You also know your spouse's boundaries and you don't intrude upon them. If your spouse doesn't like to be tickled, for instance, you know not to. To violate a clear boundary signals a lack of respect and most likely will start an argument.

We all make mistakes regarding respect and when this occurs apologies and behavior changes are in order. But sometimes there are more serious indications of a lack of respect in a marriage. This is characterized by verbal put downs (you're stupid) and open contempt for the other. But there are other more subtle forms as well. Consistently not informing one's spouse of schedule changes is one example. The most important thing about respect is a willingness to talk about it when a lack of respect is perceived. If you both affirm respect as a bedrock value, then both of you will be willing to take the time to iron out the small violations of respect when they occur. This will help you avoid the big violations of respect that can wreck a marriage.

Respect begins with respect for yourself. You cannot ask your spouse to respect you if you don't respect yourself. Self-respect grows out of our self-image, our self esteem This is why it is important for you to continually work on your own self esteem.

2. Trust

Trust is another of those bedrock values that make a marriage strong. Trust is confidence in the integrity and reliability of another person. Integrity refers to one's inner values and reliability refers to a certain congruence between what a person says and what a person does. In simplest terms, if your spouse agrees to do something for you or the children and follows through on it then you can generally trust in his or her word. Trust also has a lot to do with the sharing of information about one's schedule, day, and inner feelings. It doesn't mean that one spouse reports to another—that would make your spouse your boss. Rather, it calls for a willingness to share about one's day, life issues, and the like. Being evasive or resistant can begin to chip away at trust. Withholding information can also harm trust, as can being secretive. Abiding defensiveness can signal to your spouse that there is something to hide.

How much we can trust another is conditioned by our past. If you have had a troubled childhood where parents continually made and broke promises, then it will be harder for you to trust as an adult. And if your marriage has sustained a major break of trust, like an affair, it will be harder for you to trust again.

Above all else, trust involves a risk of vulnerability. To trust someone means that we take the risk that this person will break our heart or disappoint us in some way. When this happens we want to run, we even think about getting out of the marriage. That is why it is so difficult to rebuild a marriage when trust is violated. Apologies must be offered, anger expressed, hurt shared, and then the two spouses must commit to rebuilding trust.

A marriage can sustain a major hurt of the trust as long as the two people begin the rebuilding process and as long as the trust destroying behaviors stop. But if trust destroying behaviors continue, then the marriage can be seriously threatened.

3. Honesty

Honesty builds trust and creates respect for another person. Honesty is a curative factor in relationships because it cuts through deceit and talks about the underlying issues and the feelings present. Being honest signals to the other person that you don't want to be evasive and avoidant. Conversely, not being honest about what is happening signals that you may be willing to tolerate attitudes and behaviors that can be harmful to the relationship. Or it might mean that you are afraid to be honest about what is bothering you.

Sometimes honesty causes another to be defensive and argumentative. The best approach here is to say how you are feeling, describe the problem and its impact on you, and avoid using language of blame. You know you're using blame language when you start with the word "you," as in, "You're always. . . . " Speak for yourself, describe the problem and its impact on you and ask for an honest dialog between the two of you.

4. Safety

Safety is another of those bottom line values that we take for granted. To be safe means to be free from fear for one's physical and emotional well being. Certainly, in a relationship were there is any threat of being pushed or hit one's safety is compromised. Safety is a value that one should never have to compromise in a marriage. But there is psychological safety as well. This is the safety created that allows a person to be oneself in the relationship, free of criticism and blame. This is the safety that is built when each person agrees to refrain from criticism, name calling, put downs, and even teasing. While teasing is often fun it is a two-edged sword. It can signal playfulness but it also can communicate sarcasm and a certain degree of anger. And teasing can also escalate into a more serious sarcasm and contempt for the other. The relative degree of safety in a relationship can only be assessed by each person when you ask yourself if your relationship is safe.

Ensuring safety creates trust and loyalty to the relationship. In a society where a person's safety cannot always be taken for granted it becomes even more important for a mature marriage. In order to reach our full potential we must do so in an atmosphere where safety is guaranteed.

5. Fidelity

Fidelity is the last of the bedrock values that sustain a mature marriage. There are many meanings to the word fidelity: truth, steadfastness, loyalty, constancy are just a few. Fidelity implies at least two areas of loyalty: loyalty to the physical boundaries and rules governing your relationship, and loyalty to the emotional boundaries and rules governing your relationship. Most couples realize instinctually the need to ensure physical fidelity, meaning that one does not engage in extra-marital sexual relations with another person. What is sometimes overlooked are the rules governing the emotional boundaries of the relationship. In some marriages, for instance, it's ok if one spouse goes out to lunch or dinner with a friend of the opposite sex. But there are usually rules governing such behaviors, such as honesty concerning when this occurs and some understanding of the place. It is one thing to meet an opposite sex friend for lunch in a busy restaurant. It's entirely another thing to meet at 10 p.m. for drinks in a bar.

Marriage counselors talk about sexual affairs and emotional affairs. An emotional affair consists of a relationship with someone other than one's spouse where primary emotional needs that have been met in the marriage are now being met in that relationship. It's also possible for us to replace our spouse with work as the primary way of meeting our emotional needs. And this can be almost as harmful as an affair.

A healthy marriage is built on the two of you clarifying and communicating your bottom line values and compromising and negotiating on everything else in between. Sometimes we don't communicate these values because of fear that our spouse will not respect what we say, or because we might minimize their importance to us. By starting at affirming the value of safety the two of you can go a long way in assuring that the other values get talked about in the event that one or both of you feel disregarded. Committing to this ongoing dialog with each other is one way of ensuring that your marriage will be a place of ultimate trust and respect.

FLEXIBILITY AND COMPROMISE

Kenny Rogers sang in "The Gambler," "You got to know when to hold 'em, know when to fold 'em." In a marriage you have to know when to hold the line and when to compromise. If you know your bottom line values, those that you just don't compromise, then that means there are other issues that are open to negotiation. A major part of being successfully married has to do with the gentle art of compromise. If you're dealing with something other than a violation of your bottom line values, is it possible to be flexible? This is actually very challenging and difficult because all of us to some extent like to do things "our way." And married people often get locked into "power struggles" over issues that are really not about their core values. Maybe it's our built-in fear of domination, or perhaps we just like to spar with our spouse. But have you noticed how the little things of marriage seem to create a lot of tension? Ask yourself the next time you and your spouse are arguing "Does this issue really get at my bottom line values or is there room for negotiation and compromise?" And if there is room for negotiation and compromise, then why spend so much time fighting rather than negotiating?

A SLICE OF LIFE

Kim and Justin have been married for six years and together say they have a good marriage. But there was a time when they couldn't say this. Early in their marriage Kim had an affair with someone with whom she worked. At the time both of them had just moved a thousand miles away from their family homes and the transition to new jobs and a new location created a lot of stress. Kim's affair grew out of her own loneliness and her perceived lack of emotional support from Justin. The affair lasted for a short time, just six weeks.

When Justin found out about it he was ready to quit the marriage. But marriage counseling at that time and hard work on both their parts helped them grow steadily stronger. Justin is still quite sensitive to certain issues, like Kim going away on work related trips, or when she mentions that she has had lunch with a male coworker. Kim has made a great effort at re-establishing trust and realizes that Justin's concern and sometimes jealousy needs to be addressed. The only way around this problem, the two have concluded, is to frequently re-affirm the trust through honest dialog and a commitment to "check in with each other and check out" concerns and issues that either of them have. This process has worked up until now.

Justin now finds himself in a dilemma. A coworker who was going thorough a divorce had been confiding in Justin and the two have gotten close. She recently confided in him that she would be open to a sexual relationship with him. Justin felt guilty for allowing the relationship to progress this far; but part of him felt justified—almost as if he deserved some form of "payback."

But Justin did not want to jeopardize his own marriage. He decided to put limits on his office friendship and consulted his workplace employee assistance program, who put him in touch with a therapist. One thing became clear to him after the initial session: he still was angry with Kim for her early affair. The therapist encouraged Justin to ask his wife to do more work with him in resolving the unfinished business of their past.

In the case above there were some obvious hurts that hadn't been fully healed. They had to do with some bottom line values being violated. Yet Justin still wanted to work on the marriage, obviously because he felt that his wife was making a good faith effort at being trustworthy and respectful.

- Have there been times in your relationship when you thought one or more of the bottom line values were being called into question?

- Did the two of you commit to a process of clarifying and restating these values to one another?

- Are there any other values that you would add to the above list of bottom line values?

- Have you and your spouse ever clarified these values with one another?

The Spiritual Dimension: Letting Go of Hurt and Resentment

When our bottom line values get trampled on we often respond with hurt, anger, and distance. And we build walls and defend ourselves from being hurt again. It's an irony of married life that the person you're often the closest to can at the same time be so distant from you.

When our spouse apologizes and makes amends to us, sincerely and from the heart, it's time for us to let go of our hurt and move on. Easier said then done. Many of us keep an invisible list of hurts in our back pocket, to be used in the event that we get hurt again. The memory of the hurt lurks deep in ourselves, waiting to erupt into consciousness at the slightest hint of trouble.

Letting go and moving on can be a true response to God's Spirit moving in us. It requires some discipline and a willingness to take another risk. We are sometimes afraid that we will see in our spouse an enemy waiting to hurt us again. But in the letting go of hurt and resentment we might also be able to see an old friend, and in that old friend, the face of God.

15

Nurture Your Bottom Line Values

A successful marriage is an edifice that
must be rebuilt every day.
                                    —Andre Maurois

Understanding one's bottom line values is one crucial ingredient for a successful marriage. Taking responsibility for nurturing these values is another essential ingredient. Sometimes we have to speak our own truth concerning these values. Naming our own truth about these core values can help a couple to face a subtle erosion of their marital foundations and get their marriage back on track. It is far better to take a proactive stance toward these values by taking responsibility to see that they are actively cultivated in your marriage.

This responsibility taking can be described as *creating the core conditions* by which a marriage can grow and thrive. These core conditions are basically the bottom line values of respect, trust, honesty, safety, with one very important skill, that of empathy. Think of the core conditions as the underlying environment on which the ecosystem of your marriage will grow. If the environment is polluted and fouled then your own marital ecosystem will suffer and perhaps die. And just as we humans face the choice of taking responsibility for ensuring that the earth's air and water are free from pollution, we face the same choice in our marriage. We can create the core conditions that will sustain our marriage or we can pollute our marital environment. The following suggestions offer ways to nurture those bottom line values.

Respect

- Do focus on what your spouse is telling you by maintaining eye contact and giving your full attention.
- Don't interrupt. Let your spouse finish what he or she is saying.
- Don't invade your spouse's emotional space by insisting he or she tell you his or her every thought.
- Don't criticize your spouse in front of others, especially your children.
- Do support your spouse in front of others, especially your children. If you have a disagreement take it behind closed doors to iron out.
- Don't watch TV when having a serious conversation with your spouse. Neither of you can compete with the rapidly changing images of TV, and your eye contact will wander back to the television. This will send a mixed message to your spouse. Instead, decide on when and where the two of you will talk, turn the TV off, and then address the issues at hand.
- Don't ignore your spouse or your children. Being ignored or invisible is one of the hardest things to endure.
- Don't tease in order to communicate your displeasure. Teasing does occur in many relationships but you need to realize that it can also be a way of expressing anger and frustration. This is especially true for children.
- Do attempt to maintain the five to one rule that states for every one negative interchange between a couple there need to be five positive ones to counter the effects of the negative.

Trust

- Don't sabotage or retaliate when your spouse does something that hurts your feelings or even inconveniences you. While revenge may be fun, it hurts the trust and feels like being hit below the belt.
- Do share information about your day, your feelings, your dreams, your likes and dislikes. Information in a relationship builds trust and rapport between the two of you
- Don't see your spouse as your boss to whom you should report. This will cause resentment and you won't want to share information. Rather, see your spouse as your friend and partner with whom you have an ongoing dialog.
- Don't be evasive about your plans, whom you're having lunch with, what you're doing after work hours. If you travel be forthright and honest about where you're going, your timelines, when you will check in, etc.
- Do commit to talking with your spouse if you experience jealousy concerning relationships that your spouse has with others. Jealousy is sometimes a sign of our own insecurity and a call for us to build our own self-esteem.
- Don't engage in trust breaking behaviors where what you say you'll do doesn't match what you actually do.

Honesty

- Don't placate your spouse by saying you'll do something just to soothe him or her and then not follow through. It's better to be honest about how you feel and what you will do.
- Don't avoid conflict with your spouse. This appears evasive and can be taken as a sign that you don't want to deal with the problem or don't care about it.
- Don't minimize conflict by saying things like, "It's not that bad."
- Do say what is on your mind and how you're feeling about a given situation or problem.

Safety

- Don't respond with anger or irritation when your spouse brings issues for discussion to you.
- Do take responsibility for any anger that can be termed "explosive" where you "blow up" or go "ballistic." This type of anger makes people feel afraid and controlled by you. Your anger is yours, not anyone else's. If you are afraid of your anger then this should be a signal that safety, as a core condition, is being compromised. Sometimes counseling is required to address the underlying issues that lead to this expression of anger.
- Don't respond with sarcasm or cynicism when issues are brought to your attention. This is a subtle form of anger and can begin to undermine the safety, especially with children.
- Don't abuse alcohol and other substances. Alcohol and other substances lower your control center, thus allowing your anger to be expressed in a destructive manner.

Empathy

Empathy means "to have feelings with." To have empathy for another means that you employ your imagination to get into the "skin" of the other person, to feel what the other feels and to understand the world according to the other person's circumstances. Empathy is the life blood of a marriage because it is a learned skill that keeps the love bond strong and supple. To empathize with your spouse is to show that you care very deeply about what is going on in your partner's life. Empathy is a learned skill: it can be taught. We do this when we ask our children to imagine how another feels when that child has done something harmful.

Empathy involves, to some extent, the suspension of your own intellectual and emotional agenda so that you can better understand not only the agenda of the other, but the deeper self of the person.

Why is empathy so powerful? We know that in work groups, support groups and just about any other group there are two things that people report as being essential in making them feel part of the group. They are meaning attribution and caring. Meaning attribution refers to a person's ability to hear the deeper meaning and purpose that motivates another person. It has to do with assisting another to name experiences and dreams of the future. Caring has to do with showing another person that he or she counts and belongs.

It makes sense that marriage should be a place where two people truly listen to and help each other name their experiences. That's why we get attracted to each other in the first place, because we meet someone who is interested in understanding our deeper feelings, intuitions, and experiences. Marriage is also a place where the two of you know that you belong, that you count, and that you can turn to each other for support, care and comfort. And empathy is the skill that lets you provide meaning attribution and caring to your spouse.

Empathy demonstrates to the other person that meaning attribution and caring are high on your list. When we empathize with someone we can say "I know what you mean" by paraphrasing or restating to that person what we just heard. We communicate that we care for our spouse by trying to express the feeling we hear. While we can never know exactly how another feels, we can come closer to understanding by saying things like, "It sounds like you're feeling . . . about. . . ."

Another way we approximate the feelings of another's state is by modeling that state in our own bodies. So if your spouse is down your own expressions might appear down in order for you to communicate that you understand what he or she is going through. One of the best examples of this bodily form of empathy, though not intentional, is when a husband gains weight along with his pregnant wife, saying to her in effect, "While I can't appreciate totally what you're going through I am trying to approximate in my own body the changes I see happen in yours."

Sean sat before the marriage counselor, perplexed and stressed out. He and his wife Shelly have been married for eleven years and prior to that had lived with each other right after graduating from high school. What he didn't understand is that just recently his wife told him that she wasn't sure that she loved him anymore and that she felt that he tried to control her. As the therapist led him through an initial assessment Sean confided that in the beginning of their relationship he served as Shelly's "protector"; she had come from a physically abusive family and had a low self-esteem. Sean would bolster her confidence in the early years. But as time went on Shelly became more confident and didn't need as much protection and bolstering. And Sean's role of the protector began to shift. He became more afraid of losing Shelly and sometimes responded with anger and sometimes with jealousy when Shelly would act independently of him. Shelly told him just recently that she was afraid of his anger and that she felt controlled by it. She also entered private therapy to sort through her own feelings.

Sean and his therapist constructed an initial plan. He would work on expressing his anger in a more appropriate manner where Shelly could feel secure and safe. Additionally, he would work on his own lack of confidence and jealousy and intensity that Shelly saw as controlling. He would also try to give Shelly both time and emotional space in which to sort through her issues.

He wanted to get into marriage counseling with Shelly but realized that this would have to wait until she was ready. In the meantime the decision for him was whether he was ready to work on his own issues.

Sometimes we harm the foundations of our marriage uninten-tionally through our attitudes and/or behaviors. The important thing here is for each of you to be able to speak your mind honestly and respectfully if this is happening. It's far better to voice your concerns earlier than later. In the above case it might be too late for Sean to change, especially if Shelly doesn't want to participate with him in making the necessary changes.

- Do you think there is any hope for Sean in the above slice of life?
- Is it possible that being a "protector" of Shelly also had a darker side, one where he became controlling?
- Are the core marital conditions alive and well in your marriage?
- Are you aware of times in your own marriage where the two of you had to clarify and focus on the core conditions?
- What has been your biggest challenge to date concern-ing these conditions?

THE SPIRITUAL DIMENSION:
EMPATHY IN ACTION

St. Paul wrote about the "self-emptying" of Christ: "Though he was in the form of God [he] did not regard equality with God something to be grasped. Rather, he emptied himself . . . coming in human likeness" (Phil 2: 6-7).

Marriage often mirrors the action of Christ in that there is a similar "self emptying" process often required of spouses. We know that we are equal to each other, yet we often empty ourselves of our own needs to put the needs of the other first. We do this because of love, because of empathy for the other, whether the other is our spouse or our child.

Justice demands that the other acknowledge our equality and rights to get our needs met. Empathy encourages us not to cling to our needs in an immature grasping. Empathy moves us out of our own ego state and into the state of the other. When we say to our spouse, "I see what you mean" or "You must feel . . ." we go through a self-emptying similar to what Christ modeled. When we don't feel listened to by our spouse then the demands of justice begin to take over. Sometimes both spouses can get into a war of hurt where they compare how much they have been hurt by the other. Empathy moves our hearts to consider the hurt of the other. It encourages us to take the risk of vulnerability.

16

LAUGH HARD, HAVE FUN

Nothing was happening in my marriage. I
nicknamed our water bed "Lake Placid."
—PHYLLIS DILLER

When was the last time that you had a good laugh, a really good laugh? The type where your entire diaphragm gets involved and you're laughing so hard you almost lose your breath. Laughter is one of the best stress relievers around yet we adults often are too stressed to avail ourselves of its benefits. Children are natural laughers, always ready to share a joke or just giggle with their friends and families. A pre-schooler laughs about four hundred times per day. An adult laughs about fifteen times a day. That's quite a discrepancy and maybe explains why children often think of adults as so serious and grim.

A good joke, not a cruel one, is one that poses a problem or puzzle and offers a solution that is seemingly incongruous, yet still solves the puzzle. When your second grader asks you, "what's black and white and red all over" you might answer a newspaper, only to be trumped by the mind of your child who answers, "a skunk with diaper rash." It seems that just about everyone enjoys a good laugh.

Despite all the hassles of family life, the stress of work, the piles of laundry to do, the grass to cut, the doctor's appointments, the teacher appointments, and the worry about all that is going on in your kids' lives, it's important to realize that having fun is still a priority in your marriage. It's no wonder you're so tired and stressed, you're so busy with schedules and the like that you have almost no time for yourselves.

Marriage humor almost always has an edge to it. We can't escape it because there are so many issues to cause stress and tension and sometimes just laughing at those issues is enough to signal each other that you mean well and want to work things through. There are career issues, children issues, differences in approaches to money and finance, issues abut not getting enough emotional support, not getting enough sex, in law issues, and so on. A marriage can be so issue oriented that all the fun is driven out. Certainly, when you were courting and enjoying the fantasy of your future life together you didn't envision that you would be so bogged down with worry, discussion, and responsibility.

But our marriage humor, while often having an edge, can't degenerate into a constant barrage of sarcasm and cynicism. That signals that one's frustration with problems is moving into anger, and that anger is being directed toward your spouse. Also, there are a whole range of jokes that tend to be denigrating toward women. That type of humor is a subtle form of verbal violence against women and can be a sign in your marriage of a more serious difficulty between the two of you. The true humor of marriage allows you as a couple to laugh about the normal, every day tension between the two of you without descending into put-downs and teasing that communicates anger.

To laugh is to transcend and to transcend is to leave behind for a moment or two the troubles of life. Going to the theater, the symphony, roller blading, skiing, the ball park, out to eat, out for a movie, out with friends, and much more helps us regenerate ourselves. And it's important to make this a priority.

ARE WE HAVING FUN YET?

We all have many needs—survival, shelter, belonging, intimacy, and love. But there's another need we often leave off the list—the need for fun. In typical American fashion, you might schedule as much fun time as you possibly can. But are you really having fun, or is your leisure schedule getting you down? Some couples find themselves so busy with weekend activities that they are actually exhausted at the end of the weekend. If this is your situation, you might actually look forward to work on Monday as a place to rest!

Fun and leisure are supposed to renew us, not tax us. It's important for you to sort through those things you do that have obligation as any part of them. This gets tricky, for what might be truly fun for one of you might have some obligation in it for the other. This accounts for the arguments that you might get into over social gatherings, where one of you has a great deal of energy for the event but the other goes along with some reluctance.

To sort out what is truly fun and invigorating you might consider drawing up a "fun list." First, think of as many things as possible that you do for fun and that help you relieve your stress. (Leave off the list anything that involves the consumption of alcohol or other drugs. Any consumption of alcohol while having fun should be incidental and not essential. If alcohol is essential to your having fun then you are dependant on alcohol for having fun.)

Once you have your list, sort the list into two categories: fun and leisure that involves both you and your spouse, and fun and leisure that might involve only you. Some couples, for instance, would both play softball together, while with other couples softball might be a leisure activity of only one spouse.

Once you get your list together, sit down with each other and identify those items where you want your spouse to participate in with you. Go through your list. If there is anything that you absolutely object to doing that is on your spouse's list, you have the right of refusal. For instance, your spouse might list skiing as an activity. If you don't like to ski and are deathly afraid of doing so then that is taken off your joint list. You should have at least five to ten items on your list that you really look forward to doing with your spouse.

These now become concrete activities for you to turn to in the next phase of the process, that of scheduling in regular dates with each other. If at all possible try to go on a date with each other at least once a month. The ideal is twice a month, which would allow each of you to choose an activity from your list. By committing to creating this ritual of fun and intimacy you will gradually get into a routine where the expectation is that of fun and relaxation. But don't delay. Having fun could actually save your marriage. No joke!

Tom and Sandra had been married for twenty-four years. They have four children. Their oldest is now a senior in college. The past five years have been particularly tough on them. Their second child, a daughter, became pregnant at age eighteen, had the baby, and then married her boyfriend. And their third daughter struggled all through high school with depression. All these problems caused a great deal of stress in their relationship. Tom found himself withdrawing more and more into his work and avoiding talking over the problems with Sandra. It seemed that every day when he came home he was presented with problems. Sandra felt abandoned by Tom and angry that he had become so avoidant. She felt that he wanted her to deal with the problems and make everything right. At times she would get so angry with him that she would blow up, shout at him and criticize him.

The stress was so intense and their relationship suffered so much that at one point they even talked of separation. At that point they decided to go for marriage counseling. The therapist was able to validate Sandra's anger while encouraging Tom to face the problems more directly. And she encouraged them both to start doing more things for themselves. She pointed out that it had been nearly four years since they actually took time away for themselves. She suggested a "date night" routine where they went out every two weeks just so that they could have time away and check in with each other. At first the progress was slow, but gradually Tom and Sandra began to create more closeness in their relationship. Both are now continuing the routine of regular dates and Tom is more willing to talk about things.

AWARENESS IN ACTION

Having fun seems so obvious, doesn't it? Yet there is such a thing as "responsibility creep," where your capacity for taking on responsibility increases as the years go by. Without realizing it you can work all day, do your home chores, and attend to the needs of your children, and then have maybe a half-hour at the end of the day for yourselves.

- Is it possible for the two of you to take back some time for just the two of you?
- Finding the time when you're stressed and busy is like saving money when the budget is tight; there are few resources to go around. But if you take some time now in the midst of your business think of how much better off your marriage will be in five years when you might have more time to enjoy yourselves. So what's stopping you from having fun?

THE SPIRITUAL DIMENSION: DID JESUS LAUGH?

In the Middle Ages theologians used to debate whether Jesus laughed. There is no scriptural record of him laughing or telling jokes, although some of the stories that he told could easily have been delivered with humor. There were some theologians who were a bit scandalized by the thought of the Son of God actually laughing—as if laughter and humor were in opposition to God. There were other theologians who insisted that he did laugh because he was, after all, human.

In the Jewish scriptures when the angels tell Abraham and Sarah that they were going to have a baby, Sarah laughed out loud. She thought it was all a joke; after all she was an old woman and old women just didn't get pregnant. Later on, when she gave birth, she named the child Issac, which is a take off of the Hebrew word sahaq, to laugh or play. Sarah said on Issac's birth: "God has given me cause to laugh, and all who hear of it will laugh with me" (Gn 21:6) Somehow, through faith and perseverance, Sarah was able to transcend the shame of being infertile. She was able to laugh about it and that laughter became a fertile presence in her. So maybe God does have a sense of humor after all.

17

PRACTICE THE ART OF FORGIVENESS

The weak can never forgive. Forgiveness is
the attribute of the strong.
—MOHANDAS GANDHI

A mature marriage is built on spouses respecting and building the core conditions that create a solid relationship. But there comes a time in most relationships where the core conditions of trust, respect, honesty and fidelity will be threatened or even violated. And that brings your marriage to the reality of forgiveness. Even the little assaults to the core conditions, like forgetting to call home to say you'll be late, require to some extent the ability to seek and grant forgiveness.

Forgiveness is an art that takes practice and some discipline. It's also like eating your vegetables. You know that they are good for you and will keep you healthy long term; so you discipline yourself by eating the carrots knowing that in the long run you'll be all the more healthy and happy. While forgiveness is sometimes hard to swallow, it will keep your marital system healthy and intact through the years.

What Is Forgiveness?

In its simplest form forgiveness is the cancellation of a debt that someone owes you, whether that debt is monetary or emotional. Frederick DeBlasio, therapist and social worker at the University of Maryland, says that forgiveness is a "letting go of resentments, bitterness, and negative thinking toward someone" (*Counseling Today*, May 2000). This definition implies that someone whom you thought of as an equal has done some action that has deprived you of something of great value; that "something" can be money, bodily well being, mental health, trust, self-esteem, or much more. The perpetrator's action makes you feel resentment and hurt, and causes negative thoughts toward that person. So if your spouse has lied to you not only will you feel hurt and resentment, you will most likely think badly of your spouse. And this negative thinking ("my spouse is a liar, I can't trust him or her") will begin to shape your future response. When you forgive your spouse you experience a letting go of these resentments and negative thinking and begin to re-adjust your view of your spouse to take into account the fact that you have reconciled. This, of course, is easier said than done.

The Impact of Harmful Behaviors

When one spouse harms the marital relationship through some hurtful behavior, feelings are bruised and resentment builds. But there is a deeper impact too, the spouse who is a victim begins to experience what is known as cognitive dissonance. Cognitive dissonance results from an experience—such as betrayal of trust—that doesn't match one's beliefs concerning how another should act toward you. Whereas before there was an assumption of equality between the two people, now there is a perceived power difference. The victim feels "one down" and perceives the perpetrator as "one up." This results in a crisis of trust and a crisis of confidence. You might feel shocked, numb, hurt, or angry, especially if the offending action is a major assault on your core, nonnegotiable values and beliefs. Before the harmful event the victim could trust the spouse and felt equal; after the event there is a real lack of trust, loss of control and in a one down position felt by the victim. In order to get the relationship back on track there is a serious need for both the victim and the offender to talk things through and acknowledge the impact of the harmful behaviors on the marriage.

THE MAGNITUDE GAP

Forgiveness is easier said than done. One reason why is the gap in perception on the part of both offenders and victims. Researchers say that offenders tend to perceive their transgressions as less harmful and serious than do victims. In marriages where there is an assumption of equality between both spouses, there is a tendency for each spouse to focus more on their own victim status while over looking their roles as offenders. In other words, we tend to inflate our own sense of hurt while minimizing how we might have hurt the other person. This explains why couples can have serious arguments that go on over time and where both feel that the other is responsible for serious hurt done to the relationship. By focusing only on your role as the victim of hurt, and not taking responsibility for the fact that you can also be an offender, you might be assisting in harming your marital relationship (*Forgiveness,* McCullough, Pargament, Thoresen, editors, The Guilford Press, New York, 2000, 141).

BENEFITS AND COSTS OF FORGIVENESS

If you had to list the benefits and costs to forgiving your spouse what would they be? You might come up with the following costs of forgiveness:

- You would be required to let go of your hurt and bitterness.
- You might have to risk being hurt again.
- You would have to risk being perceived as weak, or as a "doormat."
- You would have to work on seeing the one forgiven in a way that didn't bring up all the past hurt. This can take a lot of work.

On the other hand, if you had to list the benefits of forgiving your spouse you might come up with the following:

- You really could let go of resentment and hurt and move on.
- You would enjoy better physical health. Studies have shown that harboring anger and resentment can lead to serious physical illness like heart disease.
- You might actually have more fun and enjoyment with life.
- You might see some real positive behavior change on part of your spouse.
- Your relationship could improve and deepen.
- Your spouse will cut you some slack and be more likely to forgive you should you become an offender.
- The two of you can spend much more time loving each other rather than resenting each other.

THE ART OF FORGIVENESS

Forgiveness is relational. To forgive means that you are in relationship with someone who has done something to offend you, usually an act that has harmed you at least emotionally. It's possible to forgive someone before that person asks for your forgiveness. Indeed, there have been cases where forgiveness is offered without it even being requested. One thinks of Jesus on the cross forgiving his crucifers right before he died. In a relationship between equals, however, forgiveness involves a process of dialog between the one offending and the victim of the action. That's why forgiveness is an art.

The need to ask for forgiveness and the need to forgive usually arise from a behavior that has hurt in some way the core conditions of marriage: trust, fidelity, respect, safety. Sometimes the action can be minor, like failing to call home to let one's spouse know you have to work late. The behavior can be more serious, like having an affair. And sometimes there is a repetition of minor offenses that creates a pattern of neglect, like staying out consistently after work and not checking in with one's spouse. Think of the core conditions like the bark on a tree. The tree can survive if the bark sustains slight nicks (minor offenses) and even a few major whacks by an ax (major offense), but there will come a time, if the offenses continue, that the bark will be worn away and the tree will die. Forgiveness can restore the bark on our "marriage tree."

The following is a modification of a process of forgiveness developed by Frederick DeBlasio of the University of Maryland. It asks you to address the impact of your behaviors on your marriage while encouraging you to take responsibility for an offense and let go of resentment. The language of "offender" and "victim" will be used to denote the one who does a harmful action and the receiver of that harmful action. To keep things simple we will examine the process using a relatively minor offense, a spouse who works late and does not call home to tell the other about this.

1. Clear statement of the offense

Both of you need to agree on the specific behavior that has caused a disruption in your relationship. *Victim: "When you didn't check in with me that you wouldn't be home . . . "* Here, the offense is not checking in with one's spouse. In order to go to step two the spouse who didn't check in needs to acknowledge his/her lack of action to check in. Where couples usually get stuck is when the offender minimizes his/her behavior.

2. Connecting feelings with the offending behavior

Victim: ". . . I felt hurt and angry . . . " It is important for the offender to listen carefully to the feelings of the one who has been hurt. This is not easy because the offender might think that the victim is overstating the case; and the offender has a built in tendency to minimize the impact of his or her actions.

3. Specific description of the consequence

Victim: ". . . because I had dinner ready and went to some effort to fix it." Understanding the impact that the offense had on the victim is an essential part of the forgiveness process. The offender needs to understand the consequences of the actions in the specific moment. This will assist in developing an understanding of the hurt suffered by the victim.

4. Validation of victim's position by offending spouse

Offender: "I understand and acknowledge that when I didn't call telling you I wasn't coming home that your were hurt and angry. I understand and acknowledge that you went out of your way to have dinner ready for us." Validation of the victim's position is essential in order to move on and let go. This involves a validation of the victim's feelings as well as how the offending action caused hurt and disruption.

5. Active use of empathy on part of offender to appreciate the position of the victim with reciprocal empathy on the part of the victim

Offender: "If I were in your position I would also be angry with me." Victim: "I'm beginning to understand how you react to work stress. Sometimes you get so focused and forget about me." It is important for the offender to place him or herself in the shoes of the other and experience the side of the victim. At the same time, once the offender demonstrates empathy with the spouse, it is equally important for the spouse to seek to understand any underlying patterns that might be driving the other's behavior. This is true especially if there have been serious issues like an affair, for there are often underlying negative patterns and stressors that need to be explored by either one or both of the spouses.

6. Relationship Building Plan

Offender: "In the future I will . . . do such and such to insure I check in with you. I will also take more responsibility getting organized so that I don't have as much need to work late." This needs to be very specific. It includes both how the offender will take responsibility for making amends and also a behavior change that reassures the victim that the behavior won't be repeated. Also, the victim needs to participate in the construction of this plan especially if the offense is a serious one. The relationship building plan needs to address any patterns of behaviors that might cause the action to be repeated. For instance, many people act differently toward their spouse when they are under increased work stress. They might fail to check in with their spouse. If this is a pattern then the issue will be one of doing better at relieving one's stress as part of the plan. In cases of more serious offences, like affairs, there might be other more serious patterns that cause disruption in how a couple communicates and resolves conflict. When the offense is quite serious, marriage therapy is often needed to address the process of forgiveness and to build a relationship plan that addresses all the issues. As part of the plan the couple need to address what they will do if the behavior is repeated. For instance, if the behavior is repeated again, is it time to get into marriage counseling?

7. Apology

Offender: "I'm sorry that I have hurt you by not calling." The offender at this point asks for forgiveness. Apologies can be given earlier in the process but they will be believed more deeply if the victim believes that the offender truly understands the impact of the offense on his/her feelings and also the impact of the offense on the relationship.

8. Granting of Forgiveness

Victim: "I forgive you and hope that we can avoid a repeat of this in the future." True forgiveness means letting go of resentment and anger toward the other. This can only happen if a person feels that the issue has been resolved. In serious cases forgiveness can only be given once the victim can trust that the relationship plan has been consistently followed and revised when needed. To forgive means that the victim makes a commitment not to bring up the past action again when the couple argues or has conflict. This is very difficult to do. To truly let go of the resentment and bitterness, and to see one's spouse again as a friend, partner, lover, and companion might take time, but is the goal of forgiveness. To hold onto anger and bitterness begins to make the person a real victim.

Marie and Vince have been married for seven years. Previous to their marriage they lived together for three years. They describe their relationship to their friends as close and are generally satisfied with their marriage. Life is good for them except for one thing that has created at times a great amount of conflict. Marie has at times run up her credit cards to the maximum debt limit and has lied to Vince when she has done so. Just recently a debt collector called Vince at his work and asked when they would pay back the three thousand in credit card debt that was on their cards. This caught Vince completely by surprise since he thought that they were debt free.

At first Marie denied that she had run up the debt, claiming that someone else had stolen her card numbers. Only when Vince secured a credit report did she admit the truth that she was responsible for the debt. She felt truly sorry for her actions and asked for Vince's forgiveness saying that this wouldn't happen again. This time, however, Vince found himself much more hurt and angry with Marie's actions. Further, he didn't believe her when she said that this wouldn't happen again. He felt betrayed and began having thoughts of leaving.

A friend suggested that both of them needed help and gave them the name of counselor. Marie wanted to try counseling but Vince was resistant. He struggled with his hurt and anger over Marie's actions. He eventually agreed to go with her to counseling, making no promises concerning the future.

Awareness in Action

In the above case forgiveness can be more complex than we imagine. Vince has to let go of his resentment and anger toward Marie and might have to look at whether he is taking things too personally.

- Do you think that in order for him to really forgive her he needs to see a change in behavior?

- Does it work that way with the two of you on forgiveness issues?

- Is it easy or difficult for you to forgive? What stops you from forgiving when you're hurt?

- In your experience do the issues of forgiveness involve the core conditions of marriage?

- Have you ever had to go through a forgiveness process as serious as the one described above? Do you think your marriage is in better shape because of your commitment to seek and grant forgiveness?

THE SPIRITUAL DIMENSION:
THE FORGIVING HEART

The real work of marriage begins when you are asked to forgive your spouse. Sometimes forgiveness seems counter-cultural. We are taught from an early age not to let anyone trample on our rights, to defend ourselves at all costs. And there is always the old proverb, "an eye for an eye." Wouldn't we be better off if we just defended ourselves every time our spouse did something hurtful? Yet we know that responding in kind only leads to more hostility and bitterness. But it is so hard to forgive, to let go, to release our resentment.

The root of the word conversion is "metanoia" which means "a change of heart." When we forgive another person who has wronged us we experience a kind of conversion, a change of heart. Resentment and bitterness toward another threaten to turn our hearts to stone. The conversion of forgiveness allows us to have hearts of flesh, strong and vibrant, and full of the life force of God. Forgiveness is not an easy thing to accomplish, it is normal to hold onto resentment and anger out of fear that we will be wronged anew. Forgiveness is a moment of grace where we get in touch with the fact that the offending person is a child of God just like us. Ultimately, forgiveness is a quality of God and when we forgive we assist the creator in the renewal of creation by allowing the creative energies that come from forgiveness to be released.

18

USE YOUR POWER
WITH CARE AND RESPECT

Where love rules, there is no will to power;
and where power predominates, there love is
lacking.

—CARL JUNG

In the Gospel of Matthew there is a story about the mother of James and John who wanted to insure that her two sons would have seats of power once Jesus came into his kingdom. So she went to Jesus and said, "Command that these two sons of mine sit, one at your right and the other at your left." When the other ten apostles heard about this power move they got upset, thinking they would be left out when power was distributed. Addressing the situation Jesus gave them a new teaching about power. "You know that the rulers of the Gentiles lord it over them, and the great ones make their authority felt. But it shall not be so among you. Rather, whoever wishes to be great among you shall be your servant; whoever wishes to be first . . . shall be your slave." (Mt 20:21-26). His teaching on power reversed the popular understanding of power as "lording it over" another.

What is power? Power is the ability to block or facilitate change. You know you have power over your body, for instance, when you can exercise, get in shape, and see your body change to your liking. You know that you are powerless when you contract a serious illness like cancer and feel helpless to stop its spread. You know you have power when you can influence another to do something for you. You know you are powerless when another resists and blocks your attempts at influence. This is why, for instance, parents and teens experience so much tension. The teen uses his newfound power of expression to resist the attempt of the parent to influence the teen's behaviors.

This definition speaks to both the ability to keep the status quo and the ability to change it. It provides a rather neutral starting point for our consideration of power, and challenges us to make some decisions regarding how we want to use power.

People are often queasy about talking about power, especially in relationships. Usually, talk of power is framed negatively, as when someone talks about being in a power struggle with a spouse or co-worker, or says that a person is on a "power trip." While you might be uncomfortable in discussing power with your spouse, the mere fact that you do allows you to share power rather than "have power over" another.

ASSUMPTIONS ABOUT POWER

Power Is Relational.

There is power in your relationship. How many times have you felt that you and your spouse were in a "power struggle" with each other over an issue? Have you ever felt controlled by another? It is the way we form relationships that tells us much about power. There is a big difference, for instance, in feeling like you are in an "over/under" relationship where you feel inadequate to someone's controlling behavior and feeling like you are in an "equal/equal" relationship where the two of you share power.

Power Is About Change.

Power is about the ability to change or withstand the effects of other's interventions upon us. You know that you have power when you can change things about yourself or your environment: your job, your home, things that irritate you, etc. You know you are more or less powerless when you can't change the things that are really troubling you.

Power Is About Boundaries and Limits.

Knowing your boundaries, physical, and emotional, and being able to claim them is about power. So is respecting the boundaries of another. One cultural power issue these days, for instance, is that of sexual harassment. Respecting the limits of another, physical and emotional, is a clear positive use of your power.

Power Is Something to Be Accumulated.

We wear power suits to lunches. We use phrases like "it's a war out there" to describe our business efforts. We talk of "taking power" like it was a thing to be robbed of someone. In our sports we often exalt gladiator types of athletes that seem to soar above the average person with the image of invincibility. This is a very seductive thing, because it can be manipulated by dishonest people. In this view of power there is only so much to go around, so you have to get as much as you can while you can.

A DEEPER UNDERSTANDING OF POWER

Rollo May, psychotherapist, wrote a book entitled *Power and Innocence.* He wrote this in the sixties, a time of immense cultural upheaval and change, to reflect upon how power is used for the benefit of others and how it is misused. His categories are still useful some thirty plus years later. He has five categories of power, two clearly negative, one ambiguous and two positive uses of power. All of them have an effect on how we use power in our significant relationships.

Exploitative Power

This is power in its rawest, most damaging expression. It is power against another: physical torture, abuse, domestic violence, physical violence. Exploitative power maintains an "over/under" relationship where threat and actual use of physical abuse are used to maintain relationship. This type of power is all too prevalent in contemporary marriage. It's estimated that three to four million women are battered each year by their husbands or partners, not to mention that thousands of children are subject to physical and/or sexual abuse each year. There is no excusing this form of power in any relationship.

Manipulative Power

This is power over another through the use of manipulative and controlling behaviors. Here, there is no physical violence used. Violence is present, however, in the use of threats of loss of approval, ridiculing of another's thoughts, physical or emotional state, and "thought intrusion" where a person demands to know what a person is thinking or feeling and then negates those thoughts or feelings. Information and other resources are used to maintain an over/under relationship. The person who uses manipulative power can be very outgoing and compliant with people outside the home, and even respectful of authority. But there is often present an underlying insecurity about oneself that drives a need to be in control of intimate relationships.

Competitive Power

This is power in tension with another where rules are established and where there is an underlying assumption of equality. Competitive power is ambiguous in nature because it assumes that there will be winners and losers. The American economy is built on competitive power and there can be great benefits of it.

In a marriage competitive power can be a double-edged sword. It starts from a base of equality, which is good. But if a couple is not aware of the power dynamics a competition to meet needs develops that resembles a "win-lose" dynamic. Thus, one spouse who feels that the other is not present emotionally might withdraw and withhold physically. The rules of competition state that this is a "fair" thing to do. The only problem is that instead of talking about what each person needs, and helping each other to meet these needs, a couple can become unconsciously bound by the competitive relationship game. Spouses can begin to compete to get their needs met, and this subtle competition can slowly but surely undermine the marriage. Competition for the meeting of needs often leads to hurt feelings and the classic "power struggle" that many couples often feel is present in their relationship. Competitive power is on the border line between power used positively and power used negatively.

Nurturing Power

This is power used on behalf of another person who is more vulnerable than you. One immediately thinks of the power of a mother and father who act in the best interest of their newborn baby to assist the child to reach its full potential. Nurturing power is also the power of advocacy for a person in need; care for the poor, the homeless, and those without the basic necessities are an example of this. This is the power of being an advocate in instances of life threatening situations. It's the power of taking care of someone who is clearly more vulnerable. Certainly, this is the power that asserts itself in the best form of parenting. This power also is present in the emotional caring and sharing that are present between a couple.

Nurturing power holds the vulnerably of another with tender hands, doesn't make fun of it, and protects it against the threat of any hostile force. It's the power to be present to another's pain, not to run from it, but to hold it tenderly in your hands. It is the power behind the five to one rule that we've touched on earlier. Nurturing power doesn't view the meeting of needs competitively, but actively promotes the meeting of the needs of one's spouse. This is the power to affirm and validate another in an atmosphere of safety.

Integrative Power

This form of power involves the empowerment of another person, seeing this person as capable and equal. Integrative power creates a win/win in that the power exercised fulfills both people at the same time. It is the power that allows one spouse to rejoice in the job promotion of the other, not being jealous or stingy. It is the power that allows a parent of a teenager to allow the teen to take risks and blossom, and celebrates that blossoming with the teen when appropriate. Integrative power does what it says. It integrates the different forces, temperaments, and forces present in a relationship in a way where there is a true synergy: the whole is more than just the sum of the parts. Integrative power is not afraid of differences but seeks to accept differences as adding positive value to one's own experience. Integrative power actively promotes the growth and development of the other even though that involves risk taking and additional vulnerability. This is a power that, because it is shared, creates more power. This is the power of service to others that encourages empowerment of others. It's the power of helping your spouse name his or her reality. This power is not a thing or commodity, but rather a force. In its deepest sense this is the power of the Spirit of God creating and sustaining the world.

Carla and Fred have been married for fifteen years. They have three children, ages thirteen, eleven, and eight. Both have worked full time outside the home since their third child began first grade. Up until that time Carla was a stay-at-home mom. Before their first child was born she worked as an accountant for a major health care system in town. She went back to work part time after their second child was born. She really wanted to work full time and was ready to do so, except that she and Fred would argue over her working full time. Fred was adamant that their children have someone at home when the kids came home from school. Carla agreed with this goal, except that she felt that Fred could adjust his sales schedule so that he could be home late in the afternoon. Right when she thought they came to some agreement where she thought she could expand her work hours something seemed to come up with Fred's work schedule that prevented him from following through with the plan.

It wasn't until their youngest began the first grade that Carla insisted on going to back to work full time. This created a good amount of tension in the marriage and both Carla and Fred felt at times that the other was giving ultimatums. Both had hurt feelings over the matter and both believed that each of them were the "losers" of an extended power struggle. And while they both believed in their marriage and worked on their relationship together, the topic of careers and work was a sensitive one because of the way the decision for Carla to work full time was made.

Awareness in Action

- Does this slice of life evoke any similar struggles in your own relationship?
- Have there been times in your relationship where the two of you have become competitive about certain issues or needs that you had?
- Which type of power do you strive to embody in your relationships?
- When you're stressed and tired do you go down the ladder at all to a less positive use of power?
- What do you want your spouse to know concerning how he or she exercises power in your relationship?

THE SPIRITUAL DIMENSION:
VULNERABILITY AND POWER

St. Paul was obviously a very powerful man. Some scholars refer to him as the second founder of Christianity because of his insistence that Christianity be preached to the gentiles. Other scholars speculate that he was married because at the time of his conversion he was studying to be a rabbi; at the time anyone who wanted to formally study to be a rabbi was expected to marry. Is it possible that marriage influenced his own theology and spirituality?

Whatever the facts, we know that St. Paul struggled with problems of a personal nature. In the second letter to the Corinthians he writes about a "thorn in the flesh" that he experienced (we have no idea of what this "thorn" was). He writes: "Three times I begged the Lord about this, that it might leave me, but he said to me 'My grace is sufficient for you, for power is made perfect in weakness'" (2 Cor 12:8-9). God doesn't say power is bad, just that it is made perfect in weakness.

Married people can understand this concept all too well. How many times have you had to confront your own vulnerability and to share it with your spouse. And your feelings, were they of embarrassment, frustration, anger, even shame? After all, who wants to be weak and vulnerable? And isn't it a moment of grace when your spouse doesn't reject you for being vulnerable, but encourages you to keep struggling along?

Being vulnerable doesn't mean being powerless. The task, if you accept it, is to integrate the darker, unfinished parts of you with the more together ones. When you do the work of integration, with your spouse as friend and partner, you do experience a deepening of your own power. And you discover the power of God in the process.

19

Nurture Your Inner Child, But Be an Adult

An archaeologist is the best husband any woman can have: the older she gets, the more interested he is in her.

—Agatha Christie

Marriage can be the best of times and it can be the worst of times. When things are going well we feel at our best. We can talk to each other, say what's on our mind, resolve conflict, and have great sex. But let tension and problems enter the house and things can turn sour quickly. And while we often present a calm face toward those with whom we work we are much more willing to let it "all hang out" with our spouse, sometimes to the detriment of the marriage.

In our contemporary, complex society we often show different "selves" to the world. We have our social self that allows us to meet and mingle with people. We have our work self which involves the professional roles we adopt and how we meet the expectations of the work culture. And we have our hidden selves which represent those parts of us that we don't want others to see. These hidden parts usually represent our fears, anxieties, and worries. They also show us quite clearly the underdeveloped parts of ourselves, that if others knew about, we might feel embarrassed or ashamed.

In marriage all of these selves emerge, sometimes with an intensity that we often don't expect. And when we have children all the "cracks" in our defenses seem to be exposed. Because of their energy and developmental needs children can bring out the best in us but also expose those parts of us that are underdeveloped. These are the sides to ourselves that we seek to hide from the outside world, for we are afraid of the embarrassment and possible shame that will come if people really knew, for instance, that we sometimes pout like children or throw tantrums.

A Sense of Self

Modern psychology has given us the term "ego" to refer to the self-awareness that we experience as part of our lives. According to psychologists, the ego is that part of us that is aware of the self in action and in relationship with the outer world. It gives us a sense of self and of reality, that we are different from others. It also allows for "reality testing," meaning that we often have to negotiate with the external world for how our needs will be met. Our ego also allows us to adapt to the reality before us. Imagine the young child dropped off at the day care center, deprived of its mother for the first time. That child's sense of self, or ego, must assess the threat and reach an interpretation about the events that just happened. Am I being abandoned here at the day care center? Can I meet my needs for love and care even though my mother has just left me to my own defenses? Although the child cannot verbalize these questions there is no doubt that it faces a crisis of adaptation.

The sense of self or ego continues to develop throughout childhood and even into the young adult years. It is our ego that gives us a coherent picture of the world, defends us against threats from the outside, and allows us to adopt strategies of coping and negotiating with others to meet our needs. As we grow, our sense of self adapts to the world. Thus, we can speak of one continuous sense of self or ego despite the different states we experience as we change and adapt. We often adopt different roles, behaviors, and attitudes in different situation, all of which combine to form our sense of self or ego. We can call these different roles, behaviors, and attitudes that we "try on" ego states. They allow us to continue to experiment and adapt to the world as we refine our sense of self and who we are in relationship to the external world.

THE CHILD, PARENT, AND ADULT EGO STATES

With the development of language in a young child, and as the child approaches the eighteen to twenty four-month mark there is a very clear boundary created between the child and the parent. There are a number of important developments that bring about this boundary.

The first development is that the child now has the beginnings of a verbal vocabulary that will remain throughout its entire life. Equipped now with a powerful set of words, the child can now more clearly indicate what it wants.

The second development is that by eighteen months the child has most likely made the transition from crawling to walking. This represents for the child an increase in mobility and power. Imagine your vision of the horizon expanding by double as you move up off your knees and begin looking around. Do children experience a rush of excitement at this stage? Is this like standing on Everest and surveying the entire world? We'll never know, because these experiences exist on the pre-verbal and pre-memory level.

The third development has to do with the new found power of the child to explore its world. It has to do with the child's parents using the word "no." The curiosity and newfound power of the child eventually meet up with the forceful presence of the parent.

The child begins to move about exploring the world. This movement eventually brings the child into contact with objects that the parent doesn't want touched, like books on a bookshelf. It's cute the first time an infant removes all the books on the bottom row of the bookshelf, but after the fourteenth time the parent probably has had enough. So the parent basically tells the child "no" and enforces this by some form of action, whether it's removing the child while saying "no," rearranging the room, or another form of discipline.

The effect of hearing the word "no" is perhaps the first real dawn of awareness in the child that he or she is really different and has different experiences from the parent saying "no." In a way, it's the child's first real experience with conflict. The child might respond with tears, anger, hurt, or cooperation, but the effect is the same. The no of the parent creates a boundary between the child and the parent and in effect says, "I am me (the parent) and you are you (the child)." How the child really feels about this we will again never know because almost none of us have intact memories of this first confrontation and boundary setting.

The experience of boundary setting comes back to haunt the parent, for the child eventually begins to give the no back to the parents. If the child initially feels hurt and betrayed at having a boundary created between the identity of the parent and him or herself this is often replaced by a certain power that comes from realizing that one has a separate identity. The child intuitively begins to reflect on the reality that "I am me (the child) and you are you (the parent)," but turns this around to emphasize the centrality of the child.

By saying no to the parents the child begins the dance of negotiating how one's need for love, belonging, competency, etc. are going to be met. This negotiation is not an equal one, to be sure, for parents can do very harmful things to their children. A child has no real power to stop a parent from emotional or physical abuse or from threatening to withdraw from the child if the child doesn't do as told. To realize that you are a separate being from one's parents can be a fearful thing; but it also has its rewards if one can get beyond the fear and anxiety and if one's parent's respond with a love that is stable and emotionally present to the child.

Thus, the primary ego state that we are most familiar with is that of the child since it's the first to develop. But the child, as he or she gets older, is always practicing at the two other ego states, that of the parent and adult. Children do this through their play, by playing the roles of the parent or other adult caretaker figures that our society presents to them: the doctor, lawyer, soldier, etc. As the child gets older and through the discipline of the parents the adult ego state, that of being responsible for one's behaviors and feelings, becomes gradually internalized.

By the time we reach adulthood, somewhere between the ages of twenty and thirty, we have developed sophisticated models of what it feels like to be the child, adult, and even parent. We can do this because we have experienced and observed adults and parents in action, and we have been taught how children, adults, and parents should act, and what roles they play in our society.

We bring these interactive models into all our relationships. The fun really begins when we shift into one of the ego states and begin acting out of that ego state in an unconscious or barely conscious manner.

The adult ego state—that of taking responsibility for one's behaviors and feelings and for one's participation in relationships—is the ideal for which we all strive. The issue is always one of how do we meet our needs of belonging, loving, and being loved, having sufficient power, and the like. There are appropriate and inappropriate ways of meeting those needs that have to do with the acting out of either the child or parent ego states.

DIFFERENT EGO STATES

Parent Ego State

Positive Manifestation: Includes the nurturing, supportive, encouraging, and protective dimensions of the ego. Here one takes initiative so that another's needs can be met, and voice heard, and takes responsibility for the development of another when he or she cannot assume responsibility.

Negative Manifestation: Includes critical, judgmental, and directive behavior, and all the do's and don'ts we have learned from our parents and other authority figures. Telling, commanding, giving advice when not asked, finger pointing, and scolding are all signs that we are acting out of this ego state, as is the use of "you always" and "you never" language to criticize and scold. "You're always late." "You'll never succeed at anything."

Adult Ego State

The adult ego state is the discerning part of our personality that connects feelings to behaviors and behaviors to consequences. It is the thinking part of our personality and serves as a gateway between the child and the parent ego states and attempts to balance the needs of each. It seeks to integrate the voice of the parent and child and is the part of us that takes responsibility for how we feel, think, and behave without placing the blame onto another person. Here we also take responsibility for the underdeveloped part of the child or the overdeveloped part of the parent.

Child Ego State

Positive Manifestation: The child ego state is expressed in the form of feelings. It is the emotional, fun loving, impulsive, spontaneous, sensuous, affectionate, and curious part of us. The child in us is open to new experiences and friendships. It is where we find our sense of wonder, amazement, and curiousness. It is also where we utilize our imagination to dream about what can be.

Negative Manifestation: The other side of the child can be selfish, self-centered, rebellious, aggressive, and blaming. The over developed parent will often flip into the underdeveloped child. For instance, a person can be into the parent ego state at work, come home and immediately flip into the underdeveloped child by complaining and whining about how impossible the day has been. Here one uses "you always" and "you never" language to complain about unmet needs. "You never give me a hug." "You're always so demanding."

TIPS FOR DEALING WITH THE EGO STATES

1. Above all else, strive to act from the adult ego state which takes responsibility for your feelings, thoughts and behaviors. Use "I" language: "I want to talk about a pattern that I think both of us are involved in. It may be sensitive for both of us. Can we talk about it?"

2. If you feel that your spouse is being either too "parental" or too "childish" talk about this together without using the language of blame. Realize that if you are experiencing the other as "parental," there is a good chance that your child ego state is involved in this parent-child interaction.

3. Think about why you sometimes move into the parent and child ego states. What happens to you when you're stressed and exhausted? Do you notice whether you tend to become a "child" or a "parent," either whining or taking control? The adult in each of you is capable of observing this process and understanding how to talk about what you need and how the other person can help.

4. Remember that these ego states are just that, and that the goal is to act out of the adult ego state in a consistent manner. This means that you are able to tap into the resources provided by the child and parent ego state when needed. This is an ongoing process of maturity, but one well worth the effort.

A Slice of Life

"Your problem is that you're always complaining about what is wrong with your life. You have it easy around the house. All you have to do is pick up the house, take care of the kids, and make meals."

Dan, Sheila's husband, was in high gear by the time he made this statement. This was an argument that got recycled from time to time. Sheila often felt unappreciated by Dan; she had gone to part-time work so that she could be with their young children, ages three and five. After a whole day spent with the children she would look forward to him coming home, but found herself often telling him about how difficult it was to care for two young children day after day. For his part Dan thought that Sheila had it better than him and that she complained too much.

When the argument started each of them took turns stating how much better off the other was. They would often lecture each other and point their fingers at each other as the argument escalated. Both felt that the other became too "parental" but they were at a loss as to finding a better way to argue about this issue.

It's very common to sometimes feel that you're acting "childish" and other times that you are parenting everyone in your family, including your spouse. What's more, we sometimes flip very quickly from one state to the next.

- Has this ever been your experience? Do you find yourself ever acting from either the parent or child ego states?

- Is it possible for the two of you to appreciate the positives of the parent and child?

- How easy or difficult is it for the two of you to identify the times when the negative manifestation of the parent and child ego states affect your relationship?

- What do you need to do for yourself when the negative manifestations of the child or the parent begin to express themselves?

- What do you need from your spouse when this occurs?

The Spiritual Dimension:
Playfulness, Creativity, and Responsibility

Wordsworth once wrote, "The child is the father of the man." This was, of course before inclusive language, but the poet was trying to express the romantic notion that we carry in ourselves the memory of times gone by, the memory and energy of childhood. Getting in touch with the child allows us to experience that side of ourselves that seeks to be playful and creative. Getting in touch with our parent allows us to experience that part of ourselves that longs to create a world where life and goodness can be sustained. Taken together, the child and parent in us allow us the creativity, energy and commitment to co-create the world and to contribute to solving the problems that our world faces today. The earth needs the kind of nurturing, integrative, creative, and committed energy that the mature adult possesses.

20

ATTEND TO YOUR SPIRITUALITY

Love is the only sane and satisfactory
answer to the problem of human existence.
—ERICH FROMM

The story is told of a young man who, in the days when dragons roamed the land, wished to be a dragon slayer. He apprenticed with a wise battle tested veteran who trained him and prepared him to fight dragons. On the day of his first foray the master told him, "You are now ready to face the enemy. You are prepared as no one else is, except for one thing. You need a magic word that will protect you from the fiercest of dragons." He then whispered this word to him and the young man was off. He found many dragons and was almost reckless in his battles, trusting in the magic word to give him the edge. His reputation increased with every dragon he slew. One day, a rival dragon slayer said to him in contempt, "Ha, you trust your life to that magic word given to you by your master. Don't you realize that it's only a word and that he gave it to you to trick you into believing you could fight dragons?" This caused the young man to become morose and he couldn't bear to fight anymore. He finally went to his master and asked him the truth. Alas, the master confirmed his rival's contention that the word was only meant to make him feel confident. "The important thing," the master said, "is that you trust your skills and fight on." But for the young man this wasn't enough. "Is that all there is, then, my own skills and competency? Do you mean there is nothing more?" To this the master had no reply.

The crisis of the young dragon slayer is a crisis that all of us will face to varying degrees. We want to believe that we are special and unique and that there is a protector "out there" who will see us through the difficult times in our lives. As children we are taught about benevolent figures such as Santa Claus who reward us for being good and bestow gifts on us for our efforts. It comes to no surprise to you that children's notions of God are a variation on the Santa Claus story: God is often seen as a powerful benevolent person who watches over us, protects us, and gives us good things.

There comes a time, however, when you move beyond your childhood images of God and re-appraise how you view God. This might happen when you encounter an event that shakes your sense of security: the death of a friend, parent, or sibling. Or perhaps as you matured through high school or college you got in touch with the central question that faces all believers: why do innocent people suffer if God is all powerful and good? When these experiences happen your sense of personal uniqueness and belief in an all powerful force that will protect you can fall apart, just as it did for the young man in our story. And you might have asked yourself the same question: "Is this all there is to my life, just my own experiences, skills, ambitions and dreams? Is there nothing more that transcends me?

DEVELOPING A SPIRITUALITY THAT CAN SUSTAIN A MARRIAGE

Research tells us that people who possess a well defined spirituality, and who act on this spirituality by becoming involved in a church or community setting, tend to live longer and feel better about themselves. This is perhaps because the more connected we are with other people and the more we can live out of a set of values, the more we will feel fulfilled. But this begs the question asked above: is there really anything more than just my experiences? To put it more crassly, "What does spirituality do for you anyway?"

Of course, there are never any proofs that can settle this question for you. But there are some basic instincts that you might have, that possibly point in the direction of a transcendent God. See if you, in your own experience, have the following instincts:

A Sense That Life Is Unfolding and Moving Toward a Goal

It's not that you wake up every day and know that your life has purpose. We humans are purpose seeking animals and we want to believe that somehow all things are being directed toward a goal. You might have felt this when seeking a career or in deciding what direction your life would take. Do you feel this impulse by virtue of the fact that you and your spouse have been drawn together to walk the road of life?

From the perspective of spirituality we can say that God is the unseen force directing the unfolding of life, and that God also calls to the two of you as you walk your road together.

A Sense of Mystery About Yourself and the Created World

There are two parts to a mystery: something that is known or already revealed and something that is yet to be revealed. At every stage of life you encounter yourself as mystery. When you're in grade school you know much about how smart you are and how good you are at sports. But you still have to see how that plays out in high school. When you start your career you know much about yourself, but there is also much that is hidden. Will you be successful, will you be able to fulfill your dreams, will you be happy? The same is true of your marriage. Each of you probably knows the other better than anyone else on this earth, but there still needs to be that area where both of you are seeking to discover the deeper parts of each of yourselves. Without that sense of discovery, and the awareness that there is more to learn about ourselves, life becomes stale and marriage dull.

From the perspective of spirituality we can say that God is experienced whenever we encounter the deeper mystery about ourselves and the world. Living life as a mystery to be explored rather than a problem to be solved places emphasis on inquiring more into what is unknown, both about you and your spouse. When you ponder the phenomenon of yourself, others, and the world you begin to experience the presence of God. A sense of wonder about life itself, about the fact that you can experience deeply, think deeply, and love deeply can lead you to profound transcendent experiences of God.

A Sense of Painful Life Interruptions Which Cry Out For Transcendence

The awareness of the limits of life puts us in touch with the problem of why good people suffer, sometimes quite painfully. The biggest limit is, of course, death. But there are others: loss of health, loss of job, not getting a longed for promotion, or the death of a parent, sibling, or child. Any experience with a true limit brings us up short and reminds us that we are not in control and that what we see happen to others can and probably will happen to us one day. At the same time, realizing our limits gives voice to the cry for transcendence. You see someone you love really suffer and you can do nothing about it and part of you cries out for an answer to life's dilemma: for to really live life means that one day you must surrender control. This cry for transcendence asks for reassurance that somehow one's pain, limit, death will not go for naught, that there will be some sort of return, recovery, resurrection.

In marriage the experience of limits can be very painful, for there comes a time in life with your spouse when you see the negatives as clearly as positives, your own, as well as those of your spouse. You may see, or your spouse may point out your own foibles and failings and how difficult it really is to change. With many couples, it is the experience of parenting that brings them face to face with their limits, as they struggle to deal with problems their children are facing. But in marriage, as in other aspects of life, the crucial crisis comes when one decides to face one's limits instead of running and avoiding them. The embrace and acceptance of limits can be a time of real grace and experience of God's presence even though the experience will initially be a painful one.

Scripture scholar Walter Brueggemann writes about a spiritual pattern that is captured by the Psalms. According to him the Psalms speak to our life experience of going from being *comfortably oriented* to that of being *painfully disoriented* and finally to being *surprisingly reoriented* by the action of God (*Praying the Psalms,* Walter Bruggeman, Saint Mary's Press, 1984). All of us have had experiences where life was good one day, but then the next something happened to jar us out of our ordinary and somewhat contented experience. It could be the sudden and unexpected death of a loved one, a loss of a job, a problem with a child, or even a revelation of infidelity on the part of our spouse. Whatever the event, we become painfully disoriented as our world turns upside down. We might even feel that God is punishing us or that God has abandoned us. We struggle with disbelief that the event is happening and our life enters a state of disorganization and even chaos. For some, there is a sense that life will never be the same and that the good feelings are gone forever.

The experience of becoming painfully disoriented can create a sense of crisis in your marriage. The spiritual task is to try to work it through, not running from the pain but talking through your feelings and searching for answers. If you're a spiritual person you might find that the familiar prayers and rituals no longer comfort you. The hope, of course, is that somehow in ways you don't expect you will discover that you have been surprisingly reoriented toward life. In a sense, that is the miracle of healing and letting go of intense hurt, anger, and resentment where somehow you are able to let go when before you could not.

A Sense of Being Connected With the Earth and Universe

At the giving of ashes on Ash Wednesday the minister says, "Remember, you are dust and to dust you will return." For some this is a fearful reminder of their death. But it can be so much more, for this ancient formula reminds us that we have come from the earth, belong to it, and will one day return to it. Not only that, but modern cosmologists tell us that the earth itself is composed of collected stardust formed long ago in super novae. Each of us carry in us the stuff of the primal universe and in a very real way we give voice to that primal stuff. Our brains are like quantum organisms, manipulating the molecular level of matter to produce a wonderful symphony of thought and awareness. All of which we take for granted when we debate ideas, go out for a pass in a football game, or swim at the beach. But we are children of the universe, for sure, and perhaps share a common task of experiencing life to the full and striving to allow all people on the earth do so as well.

Concerning your marriage, being connected to the earth can give you and your spouse a grounding in a sense of space. Remember that the Book of Genesis called the first man Adam, which really means, "of the earth." Perhaps the most symbolic thing both of you can do is to celebrate your "earthliness" through the act of sexual intercourse, where in the mingling of seminal and vaginal fluids you are reminded of the primal seas in which life was first created. And, of course, you know that a major goal of sexual intercourse is the procreation of offspring. As spiritual people you give rise to life in all its mystery through conception, just as the earth brings forth in mystery an over abundance of life forms.

TAKING RESPONSIBILITY FOR SPIRITUALITY

Ok, let's say you buy that spirituality is an important aspect in your marriage and that you agree with the above spiritual impulses. Are there any requirements of you? If you're really serious, there are. If you are to continue to name the mystery of God in your life, you need a framework in which to do so. Unfortunately, just the two of you will not do; you need to be attached to a community, which can give you a framework of rituals, values, and routines. In this community you can get connected with like-minded people, share experiences, and help others give voice to their own needs and cry for transcendence. And when you do take responsibility to name your spiritual reality by embracing a framework of community, you will feel more claimed by the transcendent force we call God. This might come in the form of a "conversion" experience but it also could be experienced as just being right. Remember, it's only when we try to go out of ourselves, in this case by embracing a community, that we begin to find ourselves in a deeper way. And this finding of yourself will actually strengthen your marriage and give you unlooked for strength in coping with the many limits and obstacles that come your way.

A SLICE OF LIFE

Steve and Missy have been married for twenty-three years. Their oldest is a senior in college, their middle child is nineteen and their youngest is fifteen. When their middle child, Jack was a freshman he began to experiment with drugs. When Steve and Missy found out they intervened as best they could, but Jack's problems only grew worse. He began to have more serious psychological problems which resulted in his being hospitalized when he was seventeen. He was subsequently diagnosed with schizophrenia, something that Steve and Missy were totally unprepared for. It took them nearly a year to stop blaming themselves and they gradually came to realize that his illness is a brain disorder and not the result of poor parenting.

As a result of their son's illness Steve and Missy went through major soul searching. "Why did God let this happen?" was just one question they asked themselves. Up until Jack's diagnosis they were not all that serious about attending a church. But as they began to cope with the impact of his illness they found themselves becoming more involved at a local church. For one thing, it had a support group for parents in their situation.

It also provided a strong youth group for their younger son. It's not that their re-involvement in their local church changed their lives radically. But it did provide them with a context by which they could reorganize their lives as they assisted their middle son to cope with a serious mental illness.

Life is a journey. But sometimes the highway of life gets a lot steeper and tougher than we are prepared for and life is no longer fun. Spirituality is not magic but it can give us a context in which we can ponder some of the deeper problems of life, like the problem of suffering. It won't take suffering away, but it might help you find some meaning in the suffering you experience.

- Some people have a hard time seeing themselves as "spiritual." Do you see yourself as embracing a spirituality?

- How would you describe this spirituality to a friend? Where do you find the presence of God in your life?

- Do you have specific routines, like prayer time, that help you focus on your spiritual self?

- Are there any other "instincts" or "senses" that you would add that point toward the presence of God in your life and the world?

THE SPIRITUAL DIMENSION:
IT'S A WONDERFUL UNIVERSE

The more scientists describe the created universe the more wondrous it seems. The current theory of the Big Bang holds that the universe "erupted" from a microscopic teardrop of energy-matter. Another group of scientists, in their quest for a theory that unites both physics on a large scale with physics on a small scale (quantum physics) have postulated the existence of "strings." Strings, according to this theory, are what the tiniest particles are based on. They are infinitesimally small vibrating strings of energy. These same scientist also postulate that if strings exist then there must be at least seven more dimensions.

These theories boggle the mind and seem as mysterious as the original creation myths of ancient times. While scientists can't make the leap from scientific investigation to the existence of a transcendent being we call God, their discoveries point as much toward the existence of God as away from the existence of God.

Wouldn't it be interesting if the rhythm of your marital love and the music the two of you make together throughout your married life were in some strange way related to the music of the "strings" of matter? Does your dance of intimacy reflect the dance of the universe? Aren't you curious to find out?

21

CREATE A HIGH ESTEEM FAMILY

If you've never been hated by your child,
you've never been a parent.

—BETTE DAVIS

The purpose of this book is to help you focus on and enhance your own marriage during the years when you are together raising children. If the two of you are to be equal and active partners you need more than a common approach to parenting, you actually need to enjoy your family. While it's hard to be happy every day, it's still possible to derive a great deal of enjoyment from being a parent. But you have to start with yourselves first.

Children are our greatest gifts but they are also our greatest challenges. If there are any cracks in our own personal or marital foundations, children will surely bring them out. We might escape dealing with our unfinished personal business when our children are young, but as our children grow older we will have to face them. Sometimes it seems that a teenager's main job in life is to point out our inconsistencies and to take us to our limits, by the way they behave, dress, or conduct themselves. So it behooves the two of you to understand how much of your own marital satisfaction comes from parenting well.

Virginia Satir, one of the founders of the family therapy movement in the United States, stated that the parents are the architects of the family. What that means is the way you structure your family will influence the way your children grow and mature. There are two very important factors that influence just how you will develop the blueprints for your family. These factors are Emotional Support and Structure. Each exist on a continuum from low to high and can be expressed in the form of a graph.

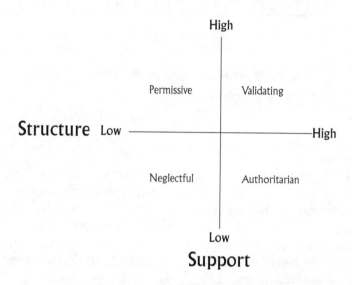

Families that are in the high structure, high support quadrant are validating families. Validating families offer children an abundant amount of emotional support along with clear expectations and fair rules. Families in the high support and low structure quadrant are permissive families. Families in the low structure low support quadrant are neglectful families where little emotional support and structure are given and children are left to fend for themselves. Families in the high structure and low support families are families where children hear more about the rules they have violated without much emotional support.

It's obvious that you want to strive to create a validating family that places emphasis on emotional support and clear expectations and rules for your children. High esteem families tend to be those families where there is a high amount of emotional support and moderate to high levels of structure. Emotional support can be defined as having the following components:

- active encouragement of the expression of feelings,
- clear and frequent positive feedback where family members know they count and know their areas of competencies,
- open communication where everyone has a voice, especially the children,
- interruptions are tolerated and everyone can interrupt equally,
- active encouragement of all members to listen respectfully,
- active prevention of the use of put downs and other behaviors that show disrespect,
- anger expressed as a feeling and not as a discipline or control device, anger is also dealt with appropriately and connected to specific behaviors that are causing problems,

Structure is also very important, but it must be flexible enough to meet the changing needs of the family, not rigid and unchangeable.

Flexible structure can be defined as:

- clear sense of boundaries where parents respect privacy of children and children respect privacy and property of siblings,
- clear sense of responsibilities and family rules,
- clear flexibility on part of the parents that signals to the children that they are approachable and open to negotiation,

- clear, not arbitrary, expectations of family members regarding chores, school, social activities, and the like,
- clear consequences and discipline procedures that are logical and consistent and understood by the child.

Additionally, as children get older they need to have a voice in helping set new guidelines based on the principle: with more responsibility comes more freedom.

HIGH SELF-ESTEEM

Dr. Gary Walz, of the University of Michigan, has written extensively about self-esteem. He claims that self-esteem is comprised of three major elements: competence, a sense of worth, and a person's own self expectations.

An individual must first feel competent in order to have high self esteem. Competence comes in three flavors. The first is functional, meaning what task you're doing. In the case of children this usually involves their school subjects, athletics, the arts and any other skill that can be learned. A person will experience a higher self-esteem based on how well he or she can master the life tasks facing him or her at that particular time in life. This explains why self-esteem fluctuates throughout the life span, since there will be times in our lives when we will be asked to master many different life skills.

The second type of competence is moral competence. This has to do with values and behaviors, being nice to others, cooperating, avoiding name calling and ridiculing of others. Teaching a child to be a moral actor in the world is a major task of parenting, and moral competence can and does create a positive sense of self in children and adults. This is why modeling behaviors such as service to the larger community needs to be part of the over all plan of creating high esteem persons.

The third type of competence is social, the ability to get along with others. It has the added emphasis on knowing the social rules of the particular group, knowing how to express oneself within the group, and generally knowing how to express and meet one's needs within the group. This type of competence addresses all the concerns parents have for their children that center around the concept of belonging and acceptance.

Self-worth is the second major ingredient to self esteem. The high esteem person is able to clearly state: "I am lovable, I deserve the success I am enjoying, I deserve the love of others, I deserve the love of self." The best environment where self-worth can grow consistently is what psychologists call the "validating family." Here messages of validation consistently come from the parents, the architects of the family.

Self-expectations form the final ingredient to self-esteem. You can think of this as one's "self talk." High esteem individuals tend to make specific statements about their failures and both specific and general statements about their success. For instance, when a high esteem individual fails at something he or she might say, "I failed today, but tomorrow I will try harder and succeed." Or when that same person succeeds, "I succeeded today because I was prepared. When I prepare I generally expect to succeed" Being very specific about success and failure allows a person to know what it takes to succeed and to stop a cascading failure message that says, "I failed at this thing, therefore I'll fail at everything." Validating families help their members develop not only positive self-talk, but specific criteria that defines success.

Some Common Mistakes Parents Make

Achieving a validating style of parenting is no easy task. It requires integration of the many different forces in us, from the negative parenting that we may have received from our own parents, to the stresses and strains of modern life. And if we have any unfinished business, our children will find the cracks in our foundation.

1. Yelling and using anger to control children

While many parents yell to enforce their discipline, you would be hard pressed to find children who enjoy being yelled at. In therapy, children tell me consistently that the one thing they would change about their family is the amount of arguing and yelling that occurs. Yelling is a form of violence in that it is usually expressed with a good deal of anger and there is always the implied threat of escalation. Yelling clearly does not validate another person but places the other on the defensive. There are ways to express your anger without raising of your voice, by connecting your feelings of anger with the behavior that is causing the problem. Yelling also tends to chip away at a child's self-esteem over time, and encourages a child to yell as he or she gets older. This is taken up in the chapter on conflict.

2. Grounding for too long or grounding as the only discipline

Parents, out of anger, often "over ground" their children, taking away privileges for up to a week at a time. Think for a moment about the word "discipline." It's from the word disciple which means one who learns. Discipline should teach a lesson and correct behavior. Many times parental discipline is more a punishment than a teaching. If your son or daughter can learn to change by losing privileges for a night or two, then why ground him or her for a week? Place the emphasis on your child learning a new behavior where the discipline is aimed at encouragement of the new behavior. The discipline should last for as long as it takes the child to demonstrate that he or she can adopt the new behavior. Here is an example of this time-oriented discipline: "When you can sit in the living room without yelling then you can join the rest of us. As soon as you begin yelling again you will have to go back to time out."

3. Inconsistent discipline without clear consequences for actions

Many times we discipline our children and then don't follow through on it. This can be true for very long disciplines, like being grounded from the TV for a week. After a while the parent who is enforcing the discipline gets tired of being the enforcer and looks the other way. It's important to be consistent in discipline. This is why the ideal discipline is usually short and inconvenient enough so as to encourage the child to adopt a new behavior.

4. Perfectionism that doesn't allow your child to fail

You may have high expectations of yourself and of your children. Indeed, if you don't expect much you often don't get much. But there is a difference between high expectations and a perfectionist mentality that requires everything to be done perfectly. Children who think they can't live up to your standards can very easily begin to internalize the "critic" within them. Or sometimes they will develop deceptive habits like lying to their parents in order to avoid either being criticized or a feeling of falling short. Children who feel they can't meet their parents expectations can begin to exhibit anger that is turned inward against themselves and also anger toward the parent who sets such high standards. Sometimes children feel that failure is unacceptable to their parents and thus will hide their own insecurities or even lie about missed homework assignments and the like. The overriding question here is whether you will love them even if they don't perform up to standards.

5. Forgetting that communication and encouragement is the first strategy of discipline

Remember, discipline means learning. Becoming an encouraging parent by validating your child's feelings, giving him or her a voice, and spending time with your child is the best way for your child to discipline him or herself. Children get validation from you by talking with you, being touched and hugged by you, and by hearing clear, specific feedback from you. When they feel ignored by you they will usually begin to agitate for your attention. With teenagers, the relationship is all important. They actually need you in their lives, but because they are much busier, you might think they are self-sufficient. Actually, they still need your validation, approval, and feedback.

6. Forgetting the contract: more freedom, more responsibility

This contract becomes activated when your child moves into the "tweens," somewhere between the ages of ten and twelve. As children move from the "latency" phase, where they are so cooperative and intent on learning, toward adolescence, they begin to want more freedom. They want to stay out later, talk on the phone more, watch more TV, and the like. Your task as a parent is to structure the conversation with them that says, "The more responsibility you demonstrate the more freedom you will be granted." Responsibility is usually defined in a dialogic process where you are talking with the child about your bottom lines (grades, respect for others, etc.) and your child has an opportunity to express what specific freedoms he or she desires. This contract will stay in effect until your child leaves home and assumes total responsibility for his or her life. Working this contract with your children is the best way to motivate them for high success.

7. Repeating or not dealing with the harmful ways we were parented

We often parent the way we were parented. Our best models for relationships come from our own families. The problem, as you well know, is that if there was any verbal or physical violence, alcoholism, or just plain neglect then those become a learning template for our own parenting. This doesn't mean that you will repeat these behaviors, but the impulse to do so is ingrained in your own brain pathways. This explains why, for instance, some people walk away from conflict with their spouse. It's often that they are afraid of the consequences of escalating conflict because they saw conflict end in violent results. So instead of risking being in conflict a person might just avoid it. We all have to come to terms with the good and the bad in our own family of origin. Sometimes we can do this by talking with our spouse, or with a good friend. But sometimes we need to commit to talking with a minister, priest, or therapist. Sometimes the issues are just too intense to sort through by ourselves.

A SLICE OF LIFE

Andy and Becky have been married for eleven years, with two children ages nine and seven. Andy is an intense but loving person who has had difficulty in the past with anger. Becky is a perfectionist who demands a lot of herself and who describes herself as a peacemaker. Both Andy and Becky come from families where one parent had a drinking problem. Andy's father was highly critical of Andy growing up and Becky's mother would become critical of her father when he drank.

Andy and Becky's pattern of arguing finds Andy sometimes becoming quite angry, raising his voice and saying "I can't believe you feel that way...." He then either interrogates Becky or starts to prove why she shouldn't feel the way she does.

For her part Becky frequently tells Andy that he falls short of what she wants from a spouse. She doesn't like his yelling and his attempts to prove that she is wrong, and she wonders if he is capable of having sympathy for how she feels.

Lately, both Andy and Becky have begun to realize that they are exhibiting toward each other the same qualities that they disliked in their own families of origin. They have resolved to do better concerning these behaviors yet become discouraged at how frequently they fall back into them.

AWARENESS IN ACTION

Children seem to bring out the best in us but sometimes also the worst. Sometimes our interactions with our children remind us of the way our parents interacted with us. Depending on your experience this can be a blessing, but it also can be a problem.

- Is there anything that you decided to change in your own parenting based on the way you were parented?
- How easy or difficult is this for you to accomplish? And have you noticed whether each of you has a different parenting style?

THE SPIRITUAL DIMENSION: VALIDATING FAMILIES CO-CREATE GOD'S WORLD

Let's remind ourselves that high-esteem families exhibit the following characteristics that remind us of the creative force of God:

- They respect the boundaries of each individual, and create safe boundaries that allow each person to express and meet his or her needs.
- They acknowledge the rights of each family member.
- There is high emotional support of family members with clear and enforced limits.
- They allow all family members to have their own voice, share their own thoughts, and share their own feelings on a particular matter.
- Clear values and expectations that can be followed are articulated. Family members are encouraged to share when they do not understand the value or expectations or cannot meet them.
- Direct and clear communications respecting feelings are the norm, and allowing individuals to take responsibility for their problems.
- They network with other families and other institutions of the surrounding culture. Healthy families know when to get help.
- They allow the individual family member to learn about how to participate in the larger culture, the benefits of the culture, and the value of respect of those of different cultural experiences.

High esteem families ultimately produce individuals who have an adequate sense of their own power, are able to create safety for themselves, feel competent in the life skills and workplace area, and have a high sense of personal worth.

CONCLUSION:
RE-IMAGING YOUR MARRIAGE

In marriage, as with life, change is the name of the game, a fact of life. We change jobs, sell homes, sometimes lose jobs, struggle to find jobs; the changes we face represent an exhausting list. One hundred years ago, change happened more slowly, and the way that people reacted to a change in their situation was conditioned by the belief that one just "muddled through." This was certainly true for marriages at that time; divorce existed, to be sure, but most people stayed married throughout their lifetime. For many in that time, leaving a marriage was just not an option when the stress of change seemed too great.

Today, of course, things are vastly different. As we move into a new century we know that our culture is a culture of both change and options. Every change creates three or four ways of dealing with that change. We are so accustomed to thinking about our options that we often become helpless when faced with the unquestioned limits of life, the most notable being the fact that we all age and eventually die.

It's clear that many people in our culture exercise their option to leave their marriages. The mentality of dealing with difficult problems has shifted, to be sure. Today, if a marriage problem cannot be fixed, there is always the option of changing one's situation by leaving the marriage. This is a fact of life and not meant to be a judgment on people who divorce; anyone who has gone through a difficult divorce knows that this choice is often the option of last resort. While divorce is an option, it is an option that comes with its own consequences for the people involved.

If change is a fact of life and if the transitions we face create tension within us and between us, divorce need not be the inevitable conclusion. We are a people of transition where change is a given. We know, too, that when we are in transition we are tested, sometimes beyond our own abilities. Even small transitions, like watching your oldest go off to school for the first time, can create within us emotional distress. And it's the way that you deal with this stress and distress that can have a huge impact on your relationship with one another.

As we have discovered through this book there are four important images or concepts that define the marital relationship: lover, friend, companion, and partner. These images represent the ideal to which a married couple strives and they represent an image of our future where we work at becoming deeper friends, lovers, companions, and partners.

It's my contention that in every significant transition that we face in our marriage the four images of lover, friend, companion, and partner must be rethought and re-imaged; and that a failure to do this can eventually be deadly to your relationship. This is because these images contain within them an imaginative vision as to how you and your spouse can meet your needs. In a sense they are archetypal images. We all need to some degree to have intimacy and to be loved (the images of lover and friend), to understand and uncover the meaning of suffering (the image of companion), and to work toward a common goal with others (the image of partner). This is why we marry in the first place, to work out very concretely how it is we will meet these needs.

But if we allow the transitions we face to thwart us, then the images of lover, friend, companion, and partner will not grow with the marriage. For example, suppose you and your spouse undergo a transitional crisis concerning a child becoming an adolescent. Suppose your adolescent has failing grades and becomes oppositional to the point that a teacher recommends counseling. And suppose that the two of you begin to argue more due to the increased stress of this difficulty. If this crisis doesn't get resolved satisfactorily, then at some level the four images of lover, friend, companion, and partner stop functioning as smoothly as they did in the past. You might even feel that you are no longer friends, or experience a dwindling of your passion for each other. You might feel that the other isn't there for you anymore, and that your parenting partnership has become strained.

But suppose that the two of you take the bull by the horns and solve your transitional crisis. As you do you will begin to understand that a strained friendship can be renewed, that you can have renewed passion for each other, that you can really be there for the other and that your partnership is now stronger. But this requires a conscious effort at re-imaging your relationship as you solve your transitional crisis. It might be hard work for the short term, but the hope is that as you re-image your relationship it will deepen and sustain you through the years.

TRANSITIONAL CRISIS

Below is just a partial list of the many transitions that we can face in our adult life. There may be others that you can add to the list. Each of these transitions take a certain amount of psychic energy to endure and to successfully weather. Not all are painful transitions and some are much more intense than others. Some you will weather just fine, others will cause more disruption. When you experience a serious disruption of your normal patterns this is a signal that the two of you may need to re-image your relationship by rethinking the images of lover, friend, companion, and partner.

Job loss

Affair

Job difficulties

Birth of child

Death of friend

Legal difficulties

First child to school

Problem pregnancy

Illness in family member

Menopause

Difficulties with a child

Relationship difficulties

Death of family member

New home

Pregnancy

Victim of crime

Miscarriage

Change in residence

Financial strain

Personal injury, illness

Change in job duties, or new job

Last child leaving home

Job promotion

Child emerging into adolescence

Signs You May Need to Rethink, Re-Image

The following represent signals that the transition you're facing is causing serious disruption in your life and in your relationship with one another.

- As a result of the transition you have experienced a loss of the sense of self. You may be more irritable, more depressed, less hopeful, etc.

- You experience an increased tension between the two of you, with more arguments that don't seem to get adequately resolved.

- There is a marked decrease in emotional and sexual sharing and more avoidant behavior between the two of you.

- You become locked into parenting roles that you don't like, such as yelling to discipline or feeling like you are "always" the disciplinarian. This may be an indication that the two of you are avoiding each other.

- You notice a decrease in emotional energy for one another and/or sexual passion. This is more than the usual decrease as a result of busy and harried schedules. ·

Re-Imaging Your Relationship

The following process may be helpful to the two of you in re-imaging your relationship as you face a transitional crisis.

1. Name the transition you are facing and its impact on you.

What is the transition? How is this transition a problem? How has it disrupted your life? Has it disrupted your own sense of self? How has the transition affected the way the two of you interact? Have you noticed an increase in tension and a dropping of the trust between the two of you?

2. Recover the energy of the original images.

Sometimes when we undergo transition we experience such a disruption in our routines that we forget about the original energy that drew us together. Try to recover some of that energy. Recall and remember the times when you experienced the energy of friendship with each other. What was that like? Recall the energy to the image of lovers. Describe the intensity and the pleasure you felt as you trusted your bodies to the other. Recall the image of companion and the times when you were there for the other when their was either physical or emotional pain. Recall the image of partner, and your dream to work together toward a common goal.

3. Re-think each image.

As a result of the transition that you have faced, do you want to continue being lover, friend, companion, and partner to your spouse? What is blocking you at this moment from freeing the energy of each of these images? Is it a lack of trust? Hurtful things that were done or said? Inattention and neglect of the relationship? Each of you describe to the other how you want to be for the other a lover, friend, companion, and partner. Describe any blocks you experience to achieving this. Ask yourself the following questions and be prepared to share your response with your spouse.

Has your friendship with your spouse been diminished or hampered as a result of what has happened in your lives? Do you want to regain your friendship if it has been diminished?

What is one or two things that you can do to begin the process?

Are you making love less as a result of what is going on in your lives? Is this the result of increased stress, hurt caused by someone's actions or other reasons? Do you want to regain the passion and energy that you lost? What needs to happen in order to do so?

Do you find yourself being less present to your spouse's personal issues as a companion? Are you focusing more on your own hurt and stress than on your spouse's? Do you want to try to be more present to your spouse? Can you name one or two things you can do to be more present?

Is your partnership with your spouse more strained as a result of what is going on? Do either or both of you feel that you are stuck in a role that you hadn't quite agreed to adopt? Is an imbalance in who does what for the household and children causing tension? Do you want to make your partnership work more to your mutual benefit? What one or two things can you do to achieve this?

4. Take responsibility for removing the blocks and recovering the energy.

Sometimes we say things that are hurtful or react in hurtful ways when we face transitions. If this is so, and you have become aware of it through this process, how will you take responsibility for the hurt sustained by your actions or words? Are apologies necessary? Is a change in behavior required? Finally, does the work of re-imaging need the help of a trained marriage therapist who can help you remove the blocks to a better marriage? If so, then exhibit the courage to say yes to this form of help.

Remember, Love Is Ultimately a Process

The deepest sense of love consists in embracing your relationship with each other as a process of continued growth, change, forgiveness, and reconciliation. When the two of you met and fell in love you became friends, lovers, companions, and partners almost automatically. You didn't have to do a lot of talking about how this happened. It just happened. That's the beauty of falling in love. But now that you are married you can experience a lack of feeling and think you're not in love. It could be that the events in your lives have burnt you out a bit and the feeling is temporarily gone. But think of the possibilities contained in the thought that you can talk to each other, share your hurt, and solve your problems together. You have to commit to this process in order for it to work. But by committing to it you guarantee your future and model for any children you have what it means to be an adult who embraces both the pain and the joy of life.

Anthony Garascia is the author of the popular marriage preparation program *Before I Do.* A marriage and family therapist in Granger, Indiana, he holds an M.S. in Counseling from Indiana University. He has been an adjunct faculty member at the University of Notre Dame and is the author of numerous articles in professional journals.